MONU-MENTAL
ABOUT
Prehistoric Antrim

TOM FOURWINDS

NONSUCH

This one's for Clive, Robert and Sheila.

First published 2008

Nonsuch Publishing
73 Lower Leeson Street
Dublin 2, Ireland
www.nonsuchireland.com

© Tom Fourwinds 2008

The right of Tom Fourwinds to be identified as the Author
of this work has been asserted in accordance with the
Copyrights, Designs and Patents Act 1988.

British Library Cataloguing in Publication Data.
A catalogue record for this book is available from the British Library.

ISBN 978 1 84588 921 0

Typesetting and origination by Nonsuch Publishing
Printed in Ireland, by Betaprint

Contents

Foreword

When choosing a county in Ulster it was tempting to look at Donegal with its wealth of megalithic tombs, or Tyrone with its wonderful selection of stone circles, but Antrim offers so much and is so rarely mentioned that it seemed like the natural choice. Monuments such as the diminutive passage tombs along the north coast, Mesolithic settlements along the River Bann, large court tombs and Neolithic axe factories give Co. Antrim in a very significant position in Ireland's prehistory.

The mountains overlooking Belfast have, because of Ministry of Defence restrictions, been off limits for many years and very little is known about the monuments in this region. Since the area was reopened to the public in 2005 local history societies have started to explore and catalogue the sites, but information about their findings is difficult to obtain at the present time. Sadly, it has not been possible to include many of these monuments in this book.

The north-east portion of the county is taken up with the beautiful Glens of Antrim, which are relatively barren on the megalithic front but do contain several important axe quarries and factories. This landscape echoes the Scottish Glens, just 20 miles from the north-east corner of the country. With Scotland so close to the tip of Antrim it is believed that the first people to enter the country arrived by this route and, when you stand on Torr East and look across to Scotland, it is easy to see why. The concentration of early sites along the River Bann does give that idea some credibility, but the lack of targeted investigation across the rest of the island does skew the statistics. The study of the Mesolithic Bann culture does demonstrate how important waterways were in allowing the early inhabitants of Ireland to access inland areas, although, again these findings could be skewed due to the fact that remains have, in the main, only been looked for along rivers where they are expected to be found.

Moving into the Neolithic era, there is a strong link between greater Ireland and Scotland in terms of tomb architecture. It was recognised that the court tomb, so prevalent in the north, shares many characteristics with tombs found in the Clyde area of Scotland. As a whole, these used to be referred to as *Carlingford/Clyde Tombs* – a moniker that has fallen out of favour. The dropping of this larger category in favour of two separate ones (court tombs and Clyde tombs) seems to dismiss and ignore the similarities purely for the purpose of isolating greater Ireland from mainland Britain. One can't help feeling that this is an act of denying an important ancient link in order to forget a regrettable modern one.

As well as the court tombs, there are a large number of portal tombs in the county, which coincide with a concentration of passage tombs across the north coast. The latter include the most northern example of passage-tomb art in Ireland at **Carnanmore** or **East Torr**, which is unfortunately all but invisible today due to erosion. In one townland, **Ballyvennaght**, there is a group of portal tombs that were all embedded up to their capstones in peat until relatively recently. Two of them, a pair that shared the same cairn, are now fully exposed. The peat here approaches 2m deep, so who knows what other wonders may lie hidden beneath it in the surrounding area?

Standing stones and stone pairs are common, but do not dominate the megalithic inventory as much as they do in some other counties. A group of standing stones around Knocklayd Mountain, including a stone pair in the churchyard in **Ballynaclogh** townland (TD), appear to try to encircle it, but there is a gap on the north-east side. If there were once standing stones around this part of the mountain, they could represent the remains of the largest stone circle to be found anywhere. Knocklayd Mountain is a round-topped, dome-like hill that dominates the northeast of Co. Antrim and can (unsurprisingly) be seen from many monuments. There are two ways to look at this: 1) it is a big mountain, so obviously it is going to be visible from a lot of places, or 2) it was seen as an important or sacred hill that was the focus of the monumental building programme in the region. Regardless of which (if either) of the above is true, the mountain is so dominant that it is hard to imagine it not playing a role.

As mentioned above, there are a large number of Mesolithic sites in Co. Antrim. These only feature in this book when they are related to other sites. As an indication of the number of known sites here is a small list: Toomebridge, Newferry, Ballyscullion, Springbridge, Mountsandel, Springhill Road, Altnahinch Bog, Cushendun, The Curran Point, Ballylumford and Glynn. Many sites line the River Bann and sites at Glenone, Fallahogey, Moneygran Bog and Mountsandel Ford add to the area's Mesolithic qualifications.[1] However, the Mesolithic inhabitants were not confined to Antrim as other short-term settlements have been found elsewhere such as Lough Boora, Co. Offaly, deep in the heart of the island.

As well as the many flint working and axe production related sites in the county, one very special item was found in the silts of the River Bann: an engraved slate plaque. These items are very rarely found British Isles but are numerous in Portugal and western Spain. Their presence in these isles has been used as proof of trade links between Ireland and Great Britain in the Neolithic period. Other examples have been found at the Neolithic axe factory at Graig Lwyd in north Wales and Glastonbury in England.

As you will see throughout this book, a great deal of work has been undertaken throughout the county by archaeologists based primarily in Belfast. Names that crop up time and time again are A.E.P Collins, E. Estyn Evans, Lawrence Flannigan and B.B. Williams amongst others. The *Ulster Journal of Archaeology* has published many excavation reports by these and other archaeologists, and these have been an invaluable resource for this book. To all these people we all owe many thanks.

Introduction

Co. Antrim's prehistoric monuments are split into two main groups in this book – *The Coastal Monuments* and *The Inland Monuments*. Apart from being convenient geographically speaking, it is also convenient in terms of monument types: the coastal regions contain a high concentration of tombs, while inland it is more mundane standing stones that dominate the listings.

The axe factories are mentioned, but have not been given as much coverage as they truly deserve. Their importance warrants a separate work and *The Irish Stone Axe Project* should become the seminal work in this regard.

Axes from the region have been found across the British Isles, predominantly in Aberdeenshire[2] (Scotland), but also as far south as Sittingbourne and Gravesend in Kent[3] (England), just as axes from the axe factories at Langdale (Cumbria, England) have been found in Ireland[4]. The trade in polished axes was extensive and possessing an axe made from a foreign material must have been very prestigious. Co. Antrim has the largest known concentration of porcellanite axes in the British Isles, which is hardly surprising considering that one of the major outcrops of the rock is to be found at Teivebulliagh.

Among the coastal monuments passage tombs are the dominant type accompanied by a smattering of court tombs, portal tombs and a wedge tomb, whereas the inland region has one portal tomb (**Ticloy** TD), several court tombs and the rest of the wedge tombs to be found in the county. A good number of the inland monuments are National Monuments and have public access, but by no means enough of them have this status. The majority of the monuments in Co. Antrim that have the privilege of being national monuments are court tombs. Those that are National Monuments are chiefly those that have been excavated. As usual, the minimum amount of land around the site seems to have been procured. This means that with some sites it is difficult to stand back and appreciate it properly – a common problem throughout all thirty-two counties. Many of the monuments would benefit from a raised viewing platform so that the monument could be viewed as a whole, as long as such a structure was clearly marked as not being part of the original monument. This platform could be a solid earthen bank rather than a wooden platform, which would save on maintenance costs and simultaneously reduce any health and safety issues.

The monuments of Co. Antrim have featured in books since Revd John Dubourdieu published *Statistical Survey of the County of Antrim with Observations of the Means of Improvement* (1811), which mentions *The Druid Stone* at **Magheraboy** TD and a monument at 'Cairngrainey', which is actually **Craigarogan** TD. The diminutive passage tomb at **Magheraboy** seems to have been the best known of the Antrim monuments during the nineteenth century, featuring in many books specifically about the county and indeed about nationwide antiquities. Borlase's *Dolmens of Ireland* (1897) mentions a total of twenty-nine monuments for the county, some of which have since been lost. Until the extensive work carried out primarily by E. Estyn Evans court tombs were referred to as stone circles due to a misinterpretation of the monuments, whereby the court was thought to be the remnants of a stone circle. In at least one case a probable ruined court tomb still appears on the OS maps marked as a stone circle (**Tobergill** TD). In 1940, *A Preliminary Survey of the Ancient Monuments of Northern Ireland* was published. This was fairly comprehensive, but over the following years several additions and corrections were published in *The Ulster Journal of Archaeology*. One monument to be omitted was the very significant court tomb at **Antynanum** TD.

The spread of the county's monuments is difficult to assess. The nature of the landscape, with its rolling glens to the east and more open flat land to the west, provides a natural division. The tombs mainly occur on the uplands between 200 and 300m above sea level. Both east- and west-facing slopes have been chosen for locations. Higher ground may have been chosen through necessity rather than choice, because the lower-lying land was heavily forested. The Neolithic inhabitants could also have chosen to live higher up for safety reasons. An extensive study of viewsheds (the area of surrounding land that is visible from a monument) may produce a pattern for each type of monument, in particular the court tombs, but some, such as **Dooey's Cairn, Ballymacaldrack** TD, are unlikely to fit into any such pattern.

When travelling around Antrim, Slemish Mountain, an exposed volcanic plug, dominates much of it and it seems like a natural focus, but many of the monuments face the coast and Slemish is hidden by intervening hills. This could be a by-product of the availability of easily inhabitable and farmable land in the early times of Antrim's occupation, but in many cases it does feel like a deliberate choice to ignore its imposing presence.

Knocklayd Mountain to the north features in the landscape of far more monuments and appears to have been used as a focal reference for many sites in the northern half of the county. Knocklayd is much more gentle and feminine in its appearance than Slemish and this may have been a factor in its attraction.

It is also difficult to escape the Mull of Kintyre, which can be seen from much of the Antrim coast. Nearly every monument that is on the east side of the glens has a view of it. On a clear day it seems to be extremely close especially from the north-east corner of the county. On the other hand, when the weather is poor it appears to be a distant, ethereal place.

The Antrim coast is well known for what are called *Sandhill* sites. These are early habitation/occupation sites that have been covered by the dunes and occasionally

Slemish Mountain.

reveal themselves after a storm. Sadly, nothing has been found as significant as the Neolithic settlement at Skara Brae in the Orkneys off the west coast of Scotland that was revealed during storms in 1850, but many important flint-working sites have been found and excavated. This book does not mention all of these sites, as there are too many to mention and they deserve a book of their own, but several interesting sites are included.

There was also an early culture based around Larne, which left a large number of crude but effective tools in what is known as 'the 25 foot raised beach' area. These raised beaches are the result of falling sea levels and rising landmasses after the last ice age. The tools were made from flint nodules, collected from the beach rather than being mined. Large portions were removed by blows to one end to produce a tapering chisel-type hand tool about 15cm long that was used for removing stubborn shellfish from tidal rocks. More refined versions of this type of tool can also be found in areas of Spain.[5]

Throughout my travels around the county, farmers have greeted me with great kindness. Access to sites has been granted without issue and they have always been keen to learn more about their monument and others nearby. I would like to take this opportunity to thank them for their courtesy and assistance; it has been a pleasure meeting you all.

Place and monument names that appear in ***bold italics*** feature in the gazetteer section. Locations outside of Antrim have the county/country in brackets after them. All other places are in Co. Antrim, but not in the gazetteer. TD is short for townland.

If you are unfamiliar with prehistoric monuments it may be worthwhile reading the *Monument Types Descriptions* section before continuing. This section describes the different varieties of monument featured in this book and outlines their defining characteristics.

About the Monuments of Co. Antrim

The Coastal Monuments

Note: *Along the east coast there is very little land between the slopes glens and the sea, so arriving at a set of criteria that define a coastal monument is quite difficult in County Antrim. Eventually, the following definition has been used – a coastal monument is one where the view is predominately towards the sea. Many of the sites along the north coast have views both inland and seawards and here a clear view of the sea has been used as the criterion. I have included some sites in this section that don't have a view of the sea, but are on the inland side of a hill with sea-facing monuments. These are included because of their likely relationship to the nearby monuments.*

Our journey along the coast starts in the hills above Belfast. Overlooking the city and offering fantastic views of it is the Cavehill National Park, a very popular place for family days out. The most conspicuous monument here is McArt's Fort, but this hillfort is too late in date for this book. However, 100m to the west of the fort is a low, denuded cairn in **Ballyaghagan** TD. The remains of this 10m diameter cairn stand no more than one metre high and the tall heather and rough ground around it make it difficult to see it properly as you approach. It is easy enough to locate though as it occupies the highest point on the hill. At the centre of the cairn it is possible to see the top edges of a ring of stones that form an internal chamber.

Looking west from the **Ballyaghagan** cairn the next peak across, Collinward Mountain, has a large transmitter mast on its summit. Next to the foot of this (and damaged by the road leading to it) there is a much-ruined cairn in **Collinward** TD. The Ulster Way footpath goes through the valley between the two peaks, but this route isn't walked very often since the metalled paths around the Cavehill National Park were constructed. If you park in the car park near the landfill site, then walking back via this old route is a much more pleasurable way to return to your car than rejoining the throng around McArt's Fort.

We now move on to the northern extremity of Island Magee, a prominence of land to the east of Larne. Here, in **Ballylumford** TD, is a much photographed passage tomb – if it wasn't so far off the beaten track it would be even better known. Only the

Ballylumford by Gray
(1883).

tomb's chamber survives. A 2m x 2m single roof stone is held aloft by four orthostats. That may not sound very impressive, but it is the monument's unusual location that makes it special: it is surrounded by crazy paving in a front yard just 2m from somebody's front door and 2m from the road. The orthostat furthest from the road is a huge split boulder with its flat side facing into the chamber.

In 1817 and 1924 *'several spiral golden ornaments and a gold collar'* were uncovered by ploughing in the fields around **Ballylumford**[6].

To reach the next site we must travel some distance north of Larne to **Ballygawn** TD, where we find an odd monument that is probably best classified as a passage tomb due to structural similarities to **Ballylumford**. For instance, the centre stone of east wall is a split boulder with the smooth surface facing inwards. The tomb, known as *Cloughogan* is now incorporated into a thick field wall next to a ruined farmhouse and was once used 'as a pigsty and poultry house'![7] Six large orthostats support a large capstone that does not quite cover the chamber. There is no backstone and rubble has slipped inside the chamber from the wall that extends in that direction. The north stone on the west side is slightly taller than the others, and a drawing in Borlase shows that the capstone was held level by a stack of stones piled upon is opposite number and a single chocking stone set on top of the taller stone. The north-south aligned chamber is 1.5m long, 1m wide and 1.4m tall. The capstone adds another 50cm to the monument's height. Towards the north end of the capstone's upper surface there are some natural solution pits, but at least two of these look very even and may have been enhanced.

A little over 1km north of **Ballygawn** in **Lisnahay South** TD there is a remarkable court tomb. The north-facing, V-shaped court is well preserved and traces of the kerb and façade can be traced. Two well-matched jambs form the entrance to a single, slightly oval chamber that is all that remains of the gallery. This chamber has been dug out to a depth of about 50cm, revealing a fine sill stone between the entrance jambs. To one side of the gallery lies a large roofstone, which, judging from its flat upper surface, lies where it was rolled off the chamber. Behind the short segment of gallery

Ballygawn from Borlase's *Dolmens or Ireland* (1897).

there are two subsidiary chambers set into either side of the cairn. The eastern one has no back stone and its walls are formed by five orthostats. The western subsidiary chamber is more complete with a backstone and an orthostat blocking the entrance. It is quite difficult to tell where the cairn ends as there are two lines of stones to the rear. This could indicate that the monument was extended at some point. Similarly, a group of set stones to the front of the gallery could be from a second court that was built in front of the original V-shaped court. The monument lies at the western edge of a wide plateau near to the base of a hill that rises 60m above the tomb. The OS map shows a stream running between the site and the base of this hill, but there is no trace of this on the ground. Being set so far back from the eastern edge of the plateau means that the coastline is out of site, but the sea is still visible.

One kilometre to the north-east of **Lisnahay South** there is another extraordinary monument: a standing stone in **Ballygilbert** TD. This is possibly the most phallic standing stone in the whole of Ireland. It stands over 1.6m tall and is 1m in diameter at the base. The top half of the stone is slightly wider. The site is on the eastern edge of Ballygilbert Hill on the Ulster Way footpath and offers spectacular views of the coast below. There is a clear view to The Mull of Kintyre in Scotland, but the top of the hill to the west blocks that to Slemish Mountain. It is also notable that Knocklayd Mountain is obscured by a hilltop rise, yet is visible from a short distance south of the stone.

Along the top of Ballygilbert Hill there are many natural rock outcrops and intermingled with these are several robbed-out cairns. It is almost impossible to tell which is which without close inspection. One fine example can be found on the opposite side of the road to the Ulster Way car park 3km south of the standing stone (this is the

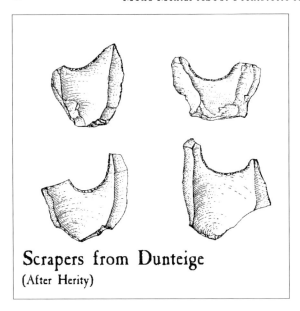

Scrapers from Dunteige
(After Herity)

Scrapers from Dunteige court
tomb (after Herity).

best place to set out from when visiting the stone.) The majority of the hilltop is good
pasture, but this does give way to some peaty marshes in places. These areas are still
very wet and possibly indicate the former presence of small loughs.

Between Ballygilbert Hill and the above-mentioned car park is Scawt Hill, the top
of which merges with Ballygilbert Hill. The 'dolmen' on Ballygilbert Hill that Borlase
describes is actually the tomb in **Ballygawn** TD (see above).

One kilometre inland from Scawt Hill is a large rocky outcrop known as Craigy
Hill. At the base of this in **Dunteige** TD are the remains of a court tomb. The monument is very ruined. Early exploration of the site by Dr J. S. Holden and Lord Antrim
around 1870[8] uncovered a large collection of flint concave scrapers[9]. A total of seventeen of these were found, as well as a large lozenge-shaped arrowhead and fragments
of Neolithic pottery, which are now in the Ashmolean Museum in Oxford, England.

Still in **Dunteige** TD, 500m to the south of the court tomb, there is a fine wedge
tomb occupying a position on a small rise with pleasant views to the north-west.
In all other directions low, rolling hills wrap around the site. The walls of the north-
east–south-west aligned gallery are in good condition, but no roofstones survive.
There is an antechamber or portico in front of the entrance, which faces south-west
in the direction of Slemish Mountain. A single, centrally placed orthostat splits this
chamber. Behind this dividing stone a septal slab blocks one side of the entrance. On
the east side of the portico a large, flat-fronted stone forms part of the façade and
there are traces of double walling along both sides. Dr. J. S. Holden and Lord Antrim
also excavated this tomb around 1870[10]. Another point of interest in the same field is
a cross-inscribed stone 100m to the east. This would have been used as a location for
Catholic masses during penal times.

In **Goakstown** TD (also known as Ault), on the west facing slopes of Black Hill 2km north of the court tomb in **Dunteige** TD, there is a large, well-preserved wedge tomb. The remains consist of a 10m long gallery made with large boulders some of which exceed 1.5m in height. Its outer dimensions are approximately 5m at the south-west-facing entrance tapering to 4m at the rear. Considering the width of the outer walling the gallery itself is very narrow at just over 1m wide. There is a single roofstone *in situ* towards the rear of the monument. A portico or antechamber is separated from the gallery by a large septal slab, which has one corner missing from it. Such features are fairly common and may have been used for access to the remains interred inside.[11] Sadly, the gallery is full of rubble and displaced roofstones, making the internal structure very difficult to see and large gorse bushes are now hiding it even further. The alignment of the gallery points in the direction of Slemish Mountain, which is very prominent from the site. This is one of many monuments 'opened and examined' by Dr J. S. Holden and Lord Antrim around 1870. At the time of these works the gallery was covered. There is a standing stone in the same townland 200m south-west of the wedge tomb.

Travelling north takes us past Glenarm and Glencloy, past Carnlough. Just inland from Carnlough is Doonan TD, where there was once a monument described by William Borlase in 1897:

> It consists of slabs lining the sides of a trench sunk in the ground. It measures 24 feet long by 7 feet broad in the centre, but narrows to a breadth of 3 feet at one end, where there would seem to have been a narrow passage forming the entrance.[12]

From this description it is hard to know whether it was a court or wedge tomb, but the accompanying drawing does look more like a wedge tomb.

Moving on around the coast we pass by Craigatinnel and Knockore Mountains. On the highlands to the south-west of these peaks there are many small loughs, which

Doonan fort and wedge tomb by Gray (1884).

must have been attractive to settlers at some period of time and these peat-covered hilltops could be hiding early settlements and maybe even tombs. The next glen to the north is Glenarriff beyond which lies the town of Cushendall. From Cushendall two glens, Glenballyemon and Glenann, cut in inland. Between them is Tievebulliagh, a steep sided mountain, which is the site of probably Ireland's most important Neolithic axe factory. The slopes below the factory are still covered with the detritus of the axe making process. The chances of finding a half-finished axe (known as a roughout) today are very slim, but this was not always the case. The scale of axe production can be understood when you consider that the person that discovered the site, William Knowles, claimed to have carried away over 4,000 roughouts.[13]

A spur of land projects outwards to the north-east from Tievebulliagh upon which there are two megalithic tombs in **Cloghs** and **Lubitavish** TDs. That in **Cloghs** TD is a southern outlier of the Antrim passage tomb group. It was once known as *Cloghancor*. This small and relatively unknown monument has a low chamber formed by five stones with an entrance gap left between the southernmost pair. Another stone stands outside of the ring of five and once formed part of the short passage. The upturned roofstone lies to the south of the chamber, left where it landed when it was cast aside. A change in the ground 3m from the chamber probably marks the edge of the cairn. To the south-west the steep-sided Lurigethan Mountain looms large, upon the flat top of which there is a large promontory fort.

Being located below Tievebulliagh obviously means that the peak dominates the **Cloghs** passage tomb to the south, but the view to the north-east is equally as interesting. Here Cross Slieve rises up above Cushendall, on the southern slopes of which there is a small hill that is shaped like a truncated cone. Its symmetry seems perfect when viewed from here.

In 1985 Wood-Martin made a passing reference to a holed stone near Cushendall: 'It is said that, not long ago, a large stone, with a hole right through it, stood on a hill near Cushendall...'[14] This referred to *The Dublin Penny Journal* in 1823 that carried a piece that included the first reference to the holed stone at Cushendall: 'it is

Cloghs passage tomb from Borlase (wrongly labelled as Lubitavish).

Cloghs passage
tomb as it originally
appeared in Gray
(1884).

said that within memory a large stone with a hole through it stood on a hill near Cushendall.'[15]

It is difficult to be sure where this stone actually stood, but the most likely nearby hilltop locations are on top of Cross Slieve, which is just north of Cushendall or atop the strange truncated-cone-like hill known as Tieverah. This hill looks very much like Silbury Hill near Avebury in Wiltshire, England – the largest manmade mound in Europe. Perhaps coincidently, there is a small pierced cross just inside the entrance to the churchyard at Layd, just outside Cushendall. The monument's record says that this stone was used as a grave marker. The stone is sandstone and may look older than it actually is as a result of weathering. Is this the holed stone that Wood-Martin referred to reused in the nearby churchyard?

S.A. D'Arcy also suggested that these two stones could possibly be one and the same in 1930:

> Dr William Frazier furnished a list of 'Holed'-stones in Ireland. Here he describes 27, all that at that time were known to him, with their localities. He states: 'No. 9, Cushendall (Antrim). – I can ascertain nothing of this stone, which is reported to have been destroyed sometime since.'
>
> While staying at Cushendall this Autumn I visited the ruins of Layde Monastery, about one mile north-east of the village. On passing through the churchyard gate, I observed in the lefthand corner of the enclosure a standing 'holed'-stone, which I then examined....
>
> The fact that the head of the stone ... is considerably wider than the shaft ... might seem to indicate that the original contour of the stone was altered, so as to give it somewhat the appearance of a rude cross.[16]

On the slopes below the **Cloghs** passage tomb there is a court tomb in **Lubitavish** TD, commonly known as *Oissian's Grave*. This is a single court tomb that faces south, towards Tievebulliagh. The wide, U-shaped court is well preserved and much of the

Tieverah Hill.

gallery structure is still present. A number of the wallstones from the gallery are missing or broken, but the jambs that marked the different segments are still in place.
These are all well matched pairs.

   To the north of Cross Slieve is the town of Cushendun. Just outside the north edge
of the town there are standings stones in **Ballycleagh** TD marked on the OS Map.
These are massive stones, each 2m tall. A third stone is said to lie in a nearby hedge.
The two stones that remain stand 5m apart just above a raised beach with a fine view
to the east that looks out to sea. 300m to the south there is a single standing stone
now standing in a flowerbed near to the reception of Cushendun Caravan Park. It is
2m tall and 1.5m wide.

   From Cushendall the A2 cuts inland and northwards towards Ballycastle.
Ballypatrick Forest lies to the west of a stretch of the road and hides two monuments
that are detailed later in the book. To the east of the A2 is one of the most densely
populated, megalithically speaking, areas of Co. Antrim. There is also a very curious
natural phenomenon: Loughareema or Loughaveema - *The Vanishing Lake*. As the
name suggests, this lough is not always full of water and is often empty. Such a strange
feature must have fascinated or even frightened the Neolithic inhabitants of the area.
The quantity of tombs in the vicinity certainly indicates that they were aware of its
special properties. The area around and to the north of the lough is **Ballyvennaght**,
a large townland with three portal tombs, a wedge tomb, at least one cairn, a court
tomb and a standing stone. A thick layer of peat covers the whole area, so there could
be many more monuments in the locality that are yet to be discovered.

The closest monuments to the lough are the court tomb, the wedge tomb and a cairn located very close to its northern edge. Both the court and wedge tombs are in very bad condition. The poor preservation of the wedge tomb makes it very difficult to find. Much of the structure has been removed, leaving just enough to enable it to be identified: a few wallstones and a displaced roofstone. The court tomb is in a similar state with a ruined gallery, displaced roofstone and two stones from the court being all that is visible.

There is a group of three portal tomb monuments 600m to the north of Loughareema. The two southernmost monuments are still buried in the peat, but the chamber of one has been dug out. The area immediately surrounding this monument has been lowered by 50cm allowing you to see the tops of the portal stones and the whole of the capstone, which is still *in situ*. The chamber is 1.5m long by 70cm wide.

To the west of these portal tombs there is one of the county's most interesting monuments – a double portal tomb – known as *Cloughananca*. Here two portal tombs occupy opposite ends of the same east-west aligned long cairn. The eastern tomb has sadly collapsed, but the other is still standing. They were once buried in the peat, but this has been dug out to a depth of 2m to reveal the whole monument. Only a low spread of stones around and between the two structures denotes the cairn and this presents an enigma. Portal tombs are often portrayed as being covered by a long cairn, or with the cairn reaching up to at least the height of the capstone. If this was the case at **Ballyvennaght**, then the cairn was robbed not long after it was built, as the cairn material was at its current level and the one tomb had already collapsed when the peat engulfed it. Therefore, it is far more likely that there was never any height to the cairn here, but that the spread of stones simply denoted a sacred area around the two tombs.

Just 700m north-west of these portal tombs there is a standing stone, also in **Ballyvennaght** TD. Overlooking a mini-valley created by several streams converging as they leave the raised area to the south, this stone is in a pleasant location with lots of atmosphere. This 2m tall stone is quite evenly shaped and is very pleasing on the eye.

To the east of the standing stone Cushleake Mountain North towers 150m above the site and to the north of this is Carnanmore, which is 30m taller. On the summit of Carnanmore, in **East Torr** TD, there is a large passage tomb. This is unlike the majority of examples found in Antrim and is more akin to those in the Boyne Valley, Co. Meath. It is also the only passage tomb in the county known to have decoration, although this is now extremely difficult to see due to weathering. However, one roofstone does have a group of clearly visible cup marks on its upper surface and these extend to the underside 'in such a position that they must be older than the construction'[17]. The cairn is 30m in diameter and 6m high. The entrance to the passage is visible on the west side of the cairn, but access to the chamber is made possible because the front section of the corbelled roof has been removed. This damage actually provides a unique chance to see a corbelled roof in cross-section. The chamber is roughly 1.5m square in plan and over 2m high.

Cloughanuncher,
Ballyvennaght by
Gray (1884).

On the summit of **West Torr**, 1.9km to the north of Carnanmore, there is another
large passage tomb that overlooks Torr Head to the east. This is in very bad condition,
but much of its massive kerb remains intact. Inside the kerb a group of orthostats from
the passage and chamber can be seen, but these are jumbled up and confusing. After
staring at the internal stones for some time and standing them up in your head it is
possible to see that this was once an undifferentiated passage tomb with its passage
opening to the north-east. The rear stone of the chamber is the only one to contain
large quartzite crystals and outside the kerb there is a large red/pink granite boulder
– again the only one of its kind at the site. On a good day the views from here are
amazing, reaching right over to the Mull of Kintyre in Scotland and the Scottish
islands. On the western slopes below the monument there are several small quarries,
the spoil of which is rich in flint nodules. It may have been these flint deposits that
attracted the tomb builders to this location.

To the west of **West Torr** is Goodland TD, where an important Neolithic ritual
site was found below the peat. This consisted of an oval enclosure with a long axis of
25m. A shallow ditch that contained Neolithic pottery and flints defined the area. In
the centre of the enclosure twenty-six pits were found that contained charcoal, flints,
pottery sherds, stones and earth. The pottery was a new type cord-ornamented ware
similar to Sandhills ware.[18]

There is a ruined court tomb in **Tervillin** TD 3km west-north-west of **West Torr**.
The damage to this monument is thought to have been done when it was 'blasted
by an inquisitive miner' in 1890.[19] The remains of the north-east–south-west aligned
gallery are poorly preserved, represented by two wallstones and one segmenting jamb.
A pile of displaced stones lies to the rear of the gallery area, where there is also an
upright stone from the kerb. The north-east-facing court is in a similar state to the
gallery with only a few stones from each arm in place, but they do allow the dimensions of the court to be estimated at about 6m in diameter. The monument stands on
a platform that protrudes from the north-facing hillside and may have been built for
that purpose. The lie of the surrounding land means that not much of the coast is vis-

Carnanmore by Gray (1884).

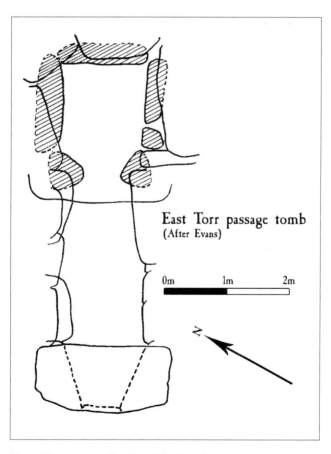

Plan of Carnanmore, East Torr (after Evans).

Cupmarks on the roofstone at Cananmore, East Torr.

ible from here, the exception being the stretch running north-west from Ballycastle
to White Head. To the south-west Knocklayd Mountain seems to sit on top of the
intervening slopes.

To the north of the court tomb, between the base of the hill and Lough na Crannagh
there is a ruined cairn known as *Cloghafadd*. This is also in **Tervillin** TD. Very little of
this site exists today after attempts were made to clear it around 1876[20]. The site is
easily visible from the road to Lough na Crannagh. Two upright stones can be seen
standing proud of a spread of rubble, presumably the remains of the cairn rather than
assembled field clearance. Of far greater interest here is the crannog that gives Lough
na Crannagh its name. This is a very good example edged with a fine stone revetment.

On the top of the hill 1km to the north-west of Lough na Crannagh, close to the
edge of tall cliffs, there is a small passage tomb in **Cross** TD. This low-lying monument
is extremely difficult to locate on the rock-strewn plateau. However, once found it is
a delight. A narrow 2m long passage leads to an asymmetric chamber that is roughly
flat on the east side, but bulges out on the west. The passage is aligned to the north
and points at the eastern edge of Rathlin Island. About halfway along its length the
eastern wall of the passage is interrupted by a stone that cuts into the passage at a
right angle and blocks three quarters of its width. A small, displaced roofstone lies in
the passage at the entrance to the chamber and a large boulder next to the chamber
measuring nearly 2m x 1.5m is presumably its original roof. Around the north-east
side of the cairn there are several stones from the kerb visible, each around 1m in
length. The site offers fine views to the west along the coast and towards Knocklayd

The crannog at Lough-na-Crannagh.

Mountain to the south-west, while Rathlin Island looks fantastic from it. The scale of this monument does not compare with those at **West Torr** and **East Torr** and is more in the size range of the small orbital passage tombs found around Newgrange and Knowth, Co. Meath. Before the top was ripped off this small tomb it was used as shelter by badgers.[21]

Another passage tomb is to be found 2km along the coast to the south-west in **Ballyvoy** TD. There are some traces of an internal structure at the centre of a well-preserved 15m diameter kerb, which is almost complete and consists of stones up to 1m in length laid on edge. It is not possible to tell from the remains which direction the passage originally faced, but it is likely to have opened northwards facing Rathlin Island like the nearby tomb at **Cross**. The tomb is located on the highest spot at the western end of the long cliffs that form this section of Antrim's coast. This gives it amazing views to the west, where Knocklayd Mountain stands proud of the lowlands that surround it. The high point on which the tomb stands is edged by a rocky cliff face just 5m from the western edge of the kerb. Below this, just 50m from the passage tomb, is the second megalithic tomb to be found in **Ballyvoy** TD – a court tomb. Only the gallery remains, but it is a massive example at 9m in length and 2m wide. The stones forming its walls are up to 2.5m in length and reach 1m in height. When viewed from the passage tomb above it appears that the gallery is aligned in the direction of Knocklayd, but this is not the case. It is aligned almost due west, whereas the mountain is to the south-west. Comparing the orthostats with the rocky slopes between the two tombs it can be seen that the stones used to build the court tomb were taken directly from there.

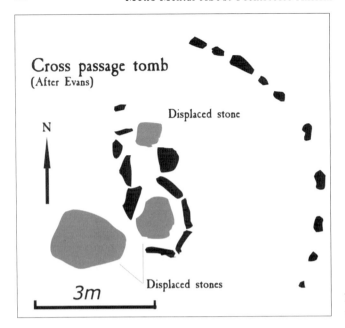

Plan of Cross passage tomb (after Evans).

There are two standing stones in the churchyard at **Ballynagloch** 1km to the south-east of **Ballyvoy**. The shortest of these is 1.5m tall and stands near to the east end of the church. The other stone is 3m tall and stands such that it greets people as they approach, or indeed as they leave, the main entrance to the church. This is one of the many examples of pagan sites being reused by later Christian churches. One thing that makes this example of reuse different from the norm is that the church is a fairly recent one. This stone pair is the northernmost stones in a group of standing stones that, on the OS map, appear to encircle Knocklayd. The stones occur around the west and south sides of the mountain and more investigation is needed to establish whether or not there were stones to the east and north-east. If these were found then it could be argued that they form the largest stone circle in Europe at over 6km in diameter. 1km to the west of the churchyard there is an artificial mound in **Broughanlea** TD.

Westward from here the coastal area is quite low for a distance of 6km past Ballycastle. It is here that Lannimore Hill reaches a height of 200m above sea level. Several place names between Ballycastle and Lannimore hill hint at missing monuments – Carnsaggart, Cloghcorr, Craignagolman, Craiganee, Carnmoon, Carnduff and Cregganboy all have references to stones or cairns. However, it is not until we come to the most telling of place names that we reach the next monument – Mount Druid.

In **Magheraboy** TD on the north-west slopes of Lannimore Hill, above Mount Druid Rectory is one of three small passage tombs that can be found in the area. This site has attracted attention since the early nineteenth century and if a book from that period onwards mentions prehistoric monuments in Co. Antrim then you can be certain that **Magheraboy** is amongst them. The site actually straddles the boundary

Magheraboy passage tomb from Borlase (1897).

between **Magheraboy** and **Ballintoy Demesne** TDs, but the site is either referred to as **Magheraboy** or *Mount Druid Dolmen* or *The Druid Stone*.

Here, a central chamber, which is open on one side, is surrounded by three quarters of a kerb. Next to the entrance is an orthostat that may be from the start of a passage. If so then the passage extended to the north. A field wall cuts across the eastern edge of the cairn and there is no sign of the kerb on the opposite side of the wall, but the excavation plan shows several large stones beneath the wall that could be part of the kerb. J. M. Mogey excavated the site in 1939 and published the findings in 1941[22].

A little over 1km to the west of Mount Druid there is another similar monument in **Clegnagh** TD. The state of preservation of this tomb is not as good as that at **Magheraboy**, mainly due to a quarry that has removed most of the hillside below it to the north. The chamber, now only consisting of two sidestones and a capstone, sits precariously on the very edge of the quarry. Gorse bushes surround the chamber now and only one of three remaining kerbstones is visible. Early sketches and reports indicate that there were once 18 stones in the kerb and that the chamber extended into the area that has been quarried away. During the fieldwork for the *Preliminary Survey of the Ancient Monuments of Northern Ireland* several pieces of flint and pottery were found in the remains of the chamber.[23]

In **Lemnagh Beg** TD (also written **Lemnaghbeg**), 400m to the south-west there is the third of this trio of north Antrim passage tombs, known as *Cloghaboghill*. This is in the same state of preservation as that at **Magheraboy**. The kerb is well represented and the central chamber still retains its 2m x 1.5m capstone. Around the cairn's circumference many of the kerbstones can still be seen, describing an area 6m in diameter. This site is less well-known than **Magheraboy** possibly because the latter's informal name (*Mount Druid*) is much more romantic, but also probably because the chamber at **Magheraboy** stands over one metre tall making it more picturesque than the still sunken chamber at **Lemnagh Beg**. Only the top 30cm of the chamber's orthostats are visible, but the inside has been cleared to a depth of one metre.

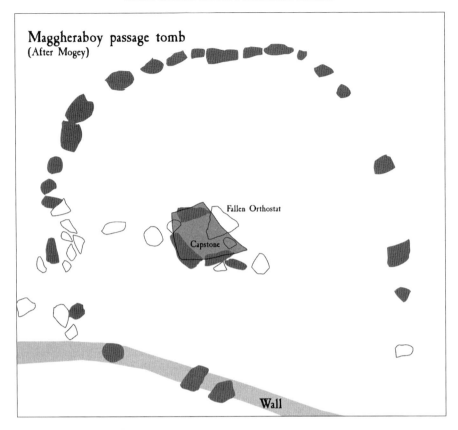

Plan of Magheraboy (after Mogey).

Clegnagh passage tomb by Gray (1884).

Lemnagh Beg from Borlase (1897).

Below these three monuments are the very poor remains of what is possibly a fourth example of a small north Antrim passage tomb, where a cairn can be seen near to the *Causeway Coastal Path* in **White Park** TD, above the beach White Park Bay. It is difficult to determine the actual size of this mound, because what appears to be the kerb is halfway up the sides of it. It may be that the monument was built on top of an outcrop in the dunes.

White Park Bay itself is a very special place, because it is to here that the rough axe blanks from **Tievebulliagh** were brought to be polished. The fast flowing streams that cross the beach and the coarse sand provide excellent tools for the job. At several places along the beach there are large concentrations of chalk boulders, some still studded with flint nodules. It was probably this easily accessible source of tool-making material that attracted people to this beach originally. It could then have become a sacred or special place associated with axe-making rituals, hence the practice of bringing the later porcellenite axes here to be finished.

The coastal fringe between these wonderful passage tombs above White Park Bay and Portrush is devoid of monuments. However, at the east end of the golf course near to White Rocks a *sandhill* site was excavated in May 1971 when a car park was constructed on a site known to contain worked flint and pottery sherds. These investigations uncovered many worked flints, part of a Neolithic polished axe, pottery and a fragment of a saddle quern. Charcoal from a hearth found in the excavation area gave a radio carbon date of 150 BCE, indicating that the site was in use over a long period of time. The most interesting find, though, was a cist burial. This was a stone-lined pit containing a flexed burial and covered with two slabs. An unusual feature of the cist was a 'tail' of basalt stones and one chalk boulder that 'contrasted strangely with its basalt fellows.'[24]

The last coastal-zone monument is a standing stone at **Ballycraig**, 0.5km south-east of Portrush. This short stone appears to have broken in antiquity and joined back together again. It is almost rectangular and stands atop a low, rounded rise.

The Inland Monuments

Having skirted around the coast of Co. Antrim to Portrush, which lies on the border with Co. Derry, it is now time to travel south back towards Belfast. The journey through these monuments will wind back and forth across the county. We start at Dunmull, an ancient inauguration site of the O'Flinns.

A little under 2km east of Dunmull there is the wonderfully named *Gig-ma-Gog's Grave*: a wedge tomb in **Beardiville** TD (see the gazetteer entry for an explanation of the site's colloquial name.) A large proportion of the gallery remains intact; the rear section of it still covered by its roofstones. The remains of an antechamber or portico can be seen in front of the gallery. Double walling can be seen along the eastern side of the gallery.

Co. Antrim's largest standing stone (by volume) stands in **Flower Hill** TD 2.5km north-north-east of **Beardiville** TD. It is 2.4m tall, 1.8m wide and 1m thick. The location is relatively high above the surrounding fields and offers a good view eastwards towards Knocklayd Mountain. The stone is rather crowded by houses and farm buildings making the views in other directions somewhat limited.

The roughly square area defined by Bushmills, Ballymoney, Knocklayd Mountain and Coraghan Mountain is heavily farmed, which might explain its relative lack of monuments. Apart from the group of standing stones around Knocklayd itself there are just three monuments in this region. In *Island Mcallan* TD there is a standing stone. One kilometre south of this there is a ruined megalithic tomb, probably a court tomb, in **Carnanmore** TD. From the road to the east this monument looks as if it is nothing more than a grassy bump in a field, surrounded by a fence. However, a line of large stones along its western side could still be *in situ*. In **Tullybane** TD, 6km south of **Carnanmore** there is another standing stone.

Around the north, west and southern sides of Knocklayd Mountain there is a dense population of standing stones. To the north there are the remains of a stone row in the graveyard of the parish church in **Ballynaglogh** TD. The tallest of these stones is over 3m tall and stands outside the church's main entrance, greeting people as they enter and leave. The other stone is at the east end of the church amongst the gravestones.

The standing stone in **Ballylig** TD to the north-east of Knocklayd Mountain equals in size the largest stone at **Ballynaglogh**, standing around 2m tall. The **Ballylig** stone is a fine example and it has been suggested that it may be the sole remaining stone from a portal tomb, but the farmer does not know of any other stones being found in the same field.[25] There was another stone of similar size dug up in a neighbouring field, however, adding to the list of standing stones around Knocklayd Mountain. A quarry marks the site of an early settlement 500m west of **Ballylig**. A Christianised standing stone was moved from the site to the opposite side of the road where it now stands, somewhat forgotten and neglected.

A little over 1km south of **Ballylig** another large standing stone can be seen from the road. This is again over 2m tall. Knocklayd Mountain dominates the site majestically. 1.5km further south in **Monanclogh** TD there is a short, uneven standing stone just 1.5m tall. This stone is crowded by a nearby hedgerow and houses to the east block most of the view towards Knocklayd. One kilometre south-east of this stone there is a ruined cashel in the same townland.

In **Knockans** TD, 1.5km south of the **Monanclogh** standing stone, there is a small one metre tall basalt standing stone known as *Clogh Berragh*. This site offers splendid views to the west and Knocklayd's presence is almost oppressive.

Directly south of Knocklayd's rounded summit there is yet another standing stone in **Breen** TD. Unusually, a tightly packed mini-cairn surrounds the base of this 1.5m tall standing stone. It is not possible to tell if this collection of stones is an ancient field clearance or an original feature. Another possibility is that the stones are actually the original packing stones that kept the stone upright in its socket, exposed by lowering the level of the field, but this is unlikely. Sadly, the view of Knocklayd Mountain to the north is not available from the stone itself due to the tall trees of a very mature pine plantation at the base of the field.

Between the **Knockans** and **Breen** standing stones there is another site of interest. Although technically outside the remit of this book it is worth mentioning because it adds weight to the argument that Knocklayd was at one time a very sacred mountain. In *Tullaghore* TD there is a very early Christian cross slab with a crudely carved knot on it. Its current position is not its original one, but it was moved there many years ago from Cullfeightrin Church on the northern side of Knocklayd.[26] Similarly, there is another crude, early cross slab not far from Cullfeitrin Church, which bears a carving of a crosier and a tau cross.

There is another standing stone 1.5km north-north-east of **Breen**, in **Corvally** TD. This is now set into a concrete base after it was knocked over by a bull. It stands on a low mound that is hardly detectable. Prior to its re-erection in 1993 excavations found that the mound was Neolithic in date, but the stone was erected later. Fragments of flint tools have been found nearby.[27]

To the south-east of Knocklayd, 1.5km due east of the standing stone at **Corvally**, there is a fine stone pair in **Duncarbit** s. Both stones are approximately 2m tall and stand 2m apart on a north-west–south-east alignment. They are said to mark the grave of John Joe McDonnell who was killed during the flight from the battle at Glenshesk in the sixteenth century. The stones are clearly older than that date, but this doesn't mean that McDonnell wasn't buried here or nearby later. The pair's alignment points not to the summit of Knocklayd, but to its northern slopes, which tantalises with the possibility of a fantastic spectacle: could the mid-summer setting sun appear to slide down the side of Knocklayd when viewed from this location?

On the summit of Knocklayd Mountain itself there is a large, oval cairn that stands over 3m tall and 25m x 30m across known as *Carn na Truagh*. Although never investigated, the monument's position would imply that it is most likely a passage tomb. A total of ten townlands meet at the summit of Knocklayd, with **Tavnaghboy** being the most commonly quoted for this site. Although no internal structure is visible, the massive stones forming the kerb around the west and south of the cairn are exposed. Unusually, these are not set into the ground, but lie at an angle against the slope of the cairn. On a clear day the views extend as far as Donegal to the west, The Mull of Kintyre to the east and the Scottish Isles to the north.

A short distance south of Dunloy off the north-west corner of Long Mountain, close to the B16, lies one of the county's more visited sites: *Dooey's Cairn* a court tomb in **Ballymacaldrack** TD. This is one of the few prehistoric National Monuments in the area and is sign-posted from the road. As with the majority of such monuments in State care, too little an area is set-aside and fenced off, making proper appreciation of the structure difficult. *Dooey's Cairn* was named after the owner of the land at the time of one of the first excavation. Professor E. Eystyn Evans, author of the wonderful *Prehistoric and Early Christian Ireland: A Guide*, carried out this work in 1935. A. Collins re-excavated the site in 1975 in order to find datable evidence. This was achieved and charcoal provided radiocarbon dates around 3000 BCE.

Ballymacaldrack's visible structure, although fairly complete, doesn't really tell the whole story. It was found that a cairn had been constructed within the court in a similar fashion to the court tomb at **Ballyutuag**, perhaps as a final sealing off ceremony. The orthostats forming the court had small dry-stone walls built between them, thus form-ing a solid wall around the area. At the rear of the slender gallery some orthostats appear to be missing, but the excavations revealed that this area had also made use of a dry-stone construction rather than the more usual orthostats. An area containing a lot of charcoal was also discovered, which was interpreted as a pyre pit – a very rare association.

The west-facing court measures 4m deep, 6m wide and is complete. Some stones from the kerb are also still *in situ* along the north side, giving the trapezoidal cairn a well-defined edge. The information signs are acceptable, but could say so much more about this fascinating site. From ground level it is difficult to fully appreciate the plan and scale of this tomb: a raised platform in front of the court would enable visitors to look down onto the monument.

Not far from the court tomb, still in **Ballymacaldrack** TD, several urn burials were uncovered when the landowner was stripping some clay in preparation for quarrying stone in 1938. This was the second time that burials had been discovered in the area. One of the urns was 30cm in diameter, 35cm tall and 'richly decorated'. Another was 20cm tall with a maximum diameter at the shoulder of 20cm. The urn with the best decoration was much smaller than these. It was just 12cm tall and had a maximum diameter of 16cm. The report of this find notes that this urn was 'not closely paral-leled among the pots in Belfast Museum.'[28]

On the opposite side of Long Mountain, 4.5km west of *Dooey's Cairn*, in **Craigs** TD is a group of three tall standing stones. Each is now incorporated to one degree or another in a field boundary. The tallest of these is over 3m high. 1km south of these standing stones, also in **Craigs** TD, is an unusual court tomb known as *The Broad Stone* or *The Broadstone*. This monument gets its name from its large, single capstone, which was removed from the monument in the early nineteenth century 'during the

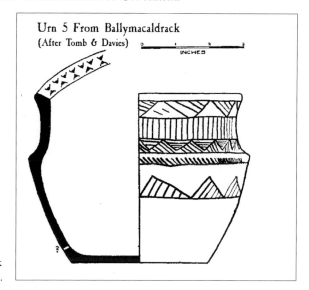

Urn 5 from Ballymackaldrack
quarry (after Tomb & Davies).

celebration of games there'[29] and then replaced late in the nineteenth century 'by the well-disposed people in the neighbourhood.'[30] Gray never actually said that the cap-stone was thrown down during games, but he did associate the site with games:

> In former times this place was resorted to on Sundays and holidays for picnics, coursing, games, and pastime, and doubtless the consequent frolic and thoughtless mirth provoked on those occasions was the cause of the dilapidated condition of this monument at present. Happily there are every few who would wantonly or maliciously destroy our ancient monuments, yet the spirit that animated the ancient Cuitech Fuait, or funeral games, has expired long ago, and the object of their com-memoration has been forgotten; therefore, the young folk of modern times, who entertain no profound veneration for ancient usages, think lightly of the injury their playfulness may occasion to ancient monuments, although, as a rule, they would not wilfully do them harm.[31]

Although in state care the site is not sign-posted, so it does not get as many visitors as it deserves. The large capstone is held up by three tall orthostats making it a very picturesque monument from the front. This arrangement also makes it look like a 'tripod' portal tomb, but it has a segmented gallery and remnants of a court.

Early descriptions of the monument have some interesting details that may or may not be taken as correct. Lewis described the site as being surrounded by a circle of stones 15m in diameter. Borlase quotes this description by Gray:

> Adjoining the cromlech proper there are the remains of three or four circular chambers, and the group of stones comprising the cromlech and chambers is again

Craigs court tomb from Borlase (1897).

surrounded by two concentric stone circles, the outer circle being 100 feet in diameter, and the inner 50 feet. Very little now remains of the outline of the circle.[32]

Nothing at all survives of any surrounding circle today. The long cairn is set in a well used field, protected by a metal fence that is (as usual) set far too close to the edges of the remains.

Gray also added that, 'the sepulchral character of the monument is proved by the finding of cinerary urns in the round chambers.' Gray's original line was slightly different, but the message was the same. It is not known what happened to these urns.

Wood-Martin gave a short, enigmatic description of *The Broadstone*, based on an article in volume two of *The Dublin Penny Journal*:

In a recess of a mountainous ridge called the Craigs…there are the ruins of a megalithic structure called 'The Broadstone.' Adjoining, is a round cavity, about 2 feet in diameter, faced with stone, and called the 'Giant's Pot'. The Broadstone marks the grave of a giant; a little to the northward three large stones are said to mark the graves of three of his followers.[33]

If this passage refers to the hollow immediately next to the remaining uprights then Wood-Martin got the dimensions very wrong, as this is over 2m in diameter. The three stones referred to are not a stone row as one might expect, but three individual standing stones in the same townland that are now incorporated into field boundaries.

In **Craigs Lower** TD, just 800m south-west of *The Broadstone*, are the remains of a very interesting passage tomb that Borlase gave the alternative name of the *Finvoy dolmen*.[34] This is an inland member of the group of coastal passage tombs that includes **Ballylumford** and **Ballyboley**. The tomb is situated on west-facing slopes with fine views over Co. Londonderry/Derry. Its single capstone is supported by seven slender orthostats on an east-west alignment, with the entrance facing west. There is a gap in the orthostats on the north side where a stone has been removed. In front of the entrance there is a low stone that once formed part of a short passage.

In 1883 Gray wrote that, 'Formerly this monument was almost covered by earth, the cap-stone alone being exposed. The earth was removed some years ago, and the monument now stands on the natural ground surface.'[35]

The tomb remained in this state until 1976/77 when the capstone was shattered into five pieces by heavy frosts.[36] In 1982 the monument passed into state care and B. Williams undertook an excavation in 1985 prior to the replacement of the capstone and of an orthostat that had also fallen. A radiocarbon date was obtained from oak charcoal of approximately 1400 BCE. Williams noted that this date was probably from a secondary deposit and 'is clearly not associated with the construction of this tomb, which on comparative grounds might reasonably be expected to date to the third millennium B.C.' and that it could relate to an urn that Gray reported being found inside the chamber.[37]

Moving east past Clogh Mills a number of rivers converge to form Clogh River. These tributaries (amongst them Ballsallagh Water, Skerry Water and Glenravel Water) have carved a valley that runs from north-east to south-west into the plains of central Antrim. Bush River rises just one kilometre from the head of Skerry Water and makes its way north to Bushmills. Around the Clogh River valley there are many standing stones, the largest concentration in Antrim.

Two adjacent townlands in the valley, Tullykittagh Lower and Upper Tullykittagh, had an impressive list of sites recorded in the OS memoirs. The records in the *Northern*

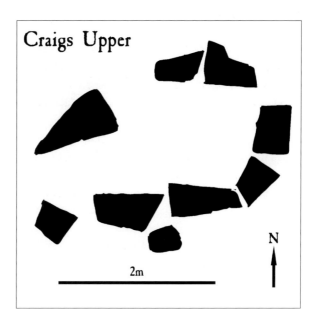

Plan of Craigs Upper (after Williams).

Craigs Lower from Borlase (1897).

Ireland Sites and Monuments Record tell a sad tale. It lists eight standing stones, nine megalithic tombs, two cairns and a stone circle, none of which remain today. An urn burial was found in 1836 in one of these townlands.

To the north of Tullykittagh there is a standing stone in **Scotchomerbane** TD. This is now incorporated into a roadside dry-stone wall. It stands just under 2m tall and has a slight groove in its top.

To the south-east of **Scotchomerbane** there is another standing stone in **Skerry West** TD, located near to a crossroads. This stone has a groove running across its top and stands around 2m tall. One kilometre further to the south-east is a stone pair in **Lisnamanny** TD. A track has been driven between these two 1.5m tall stones, making them look like gateposts.

Further up the valley to the south-east of **Cargan** there is a large standing stone that is sandwiched between a new house and a garage. It is around 1.8m tall and 1.5m wide. If this is the standing stone marked on the OS map, then it appears to either have been moved or it was marked in the wrong location. It now acts as a large garden feature.

The Clogh River valley is overlooked from the south by Carncormick Mountain, which has a low cairn at its summit.

The next valley to the south is formed by Braid River, which eventually passes through Ballymena. This valley is overlooked from the south by Slemish Mountain, an impressive exposed volcanic plug. Like the Clogh River valley this too runs from north-east to south-west.

Not marked on the OS map there is a standing stone at the head of this valley, 3km north of Ballymena in **Craigywarren** TD. This is an unimpressive stone a little over 1m tall. One thing in its favour is the impressive view it has to the east, along the valley towards Slemish Mountain.

On the northern slopes of the valley, 7km east of *Craigywarren*, is Skerry Rock, an ancient church site. This stands on the top of a rocky eminence that offers tremendous views of the valley and in particular across the valley to Slemish. It is said that St Patrick tried to step from this rocky platform on to the top of Slemish Mounatin, but failed. A stone near the church marks the spot where he stood to make this giant stride and there is a depression in this stone that is said to be his footprint. Another stone in the valley below has a similar depression that is supposed to be the footprint he left when he landed after failing to step onto Slemish. This tale is very similar to other, older tales of giants and hags striding from mountaintop to mountaintop and failing. It can be argued that these stories are very ancient and that the attributing of this one to Patrick is an attempt to steal it from pagan myth. What is surprising, though, is that St Patrick still failed in his attempt, rather than succeeding where others failed.

In the noon shadow of the rock on which Skerry church now stands there are the remains of a very ruined and very well disguised court tomb in *Loughconnelly* TD. This site is so well hidden that the *Northern Ireland Sites and Monuments Record* lists it as destroyed. The 1940 record of the site described it as having two 2m tall stones at the east end and a 'single-chambered grave (opening) towards the longer (N.) side of the cairn'.[38] The single-chambered grave mentioned is not visible today, but the two 2m stones are still exposed alongside a well-maintained farm track. The cairn still reaches over 2m high, but a 1.5m tall dry-stone wall edges it, making it blend in with the surrounding field boundaries.

Near to the head of the valley, 5km east of *Loughconnelly*, there is an ungainly-looking portal tomb in *Ticloy* TD, known as *The Stone House*. It is constructed of very large and ugly blocks of stone. The capstone is still *in situ* but has cracked across its width and one of the portal stones has fallen. Despite being possibly the ugliest example in the whole of Ireland of these usually picturesque monuments, it is an interesting one. Borlase quoted a lengthy description of the monument by F. Stokes that mentions a second structure to the rear (west) of the one that remains:

> On the western side there is a second Stone House. It is lower than the first, the stones being at an average but 2 feet above the ground, and it also wants a roof. Attached is another platform of stones, having the average altitude above the level of the field.
>
> In one of the stone dykes of the same field there is a large block of stone, originally found lying near the second monument. Its dimensions are: length, 6 feet; breadth, 3 feet; and thickness from 1 foot to 1 foot 6 ins. Its form is regular. It evidently had been once the covering-stone for it. The tenant relates that before it was removed to the dyke, it had stood time out of mind close to the eastern side of the 'House'. It rested on its edge, and was propped up by small stones, so as to form an angle of 45° with the horizon.[39]

The large stone mentioned can still be seen in a field wall between a farm track and the field containing the portal tomb. Stokes also said that the tomb stood 'at the head of a long platform, which is raised about 2 feet above the level of the surrounding field.' No sign of this long cairn remains today. It was presumably ploughed out at the same time as the removal of the second structure.

When Borlase visited the monument he noted that, 'the roof was covered with stones, thrown there…not by mere accident, but in accordance with some dimly remembered superstition.'[40] This is not the only superstition regarding throwing stones onto the capstone of a portal tomb. At Proleek, Co. Louth, people used to throw stones onto its round-topped capstone. If your stone did not fall off, it was said that you would be married within the year.

The drawing of **Ticloy** in Borlase's *Dolmens of Ireland* and the one in Gray's 1884 report[41] show a low stone next to the northern portal stone. This stone can still be seen, but it no longer stands upright. The remains of a shallow court that once stood in front of the tomb entrance, again outlining the link between portal and court tombs. Gray's drawing also features the second structure.

It is most unfortunate that Borlase did not visit another monument in the area that he mentions in passing:

> On the heath above these dolmens is a stone circle enclosing a chamber measuring 6 feet by 5 feet, and having an avenue, or passage, at one end, measuring 6 feet by 2 feet.[42]

This monument would now appear to be lost and, from this description, was almost certainly a passage tomb. The report from an excursion in 1883 by some members of *The Royal and Historical Society of Ireland* also mentions this site:

> Passing Longmore, "the large fortification," and turning a mountainous road to the right, between Claggan and Clough, we observed a large stone circle on the heath of Little Ballymenagh Mountain.[43]

Ticloy portal tomb by Gray (1884).

Ticloy portal tomb from Borlase (1897).

To the south-east of **Ticloy** lies **Antynanum** or **Antananum** townland, which is still rich in remains. Two kilometres from **Ticloy** there is the first of two stone pairs. These stand at the base of a steep slope on the floodplain of the Braid. The other stone pair in this large townland is 1.1km south-east of these and is known as *The Maidens*. These stones are about 1.5m tall and stand 5m apart. They are unusually located in a depression between a slope and small knoll with limited views.

Between the two stone pairs is a wonderful court tomb that has escaped much attention due to not being marked on the OS maps. Its cairn is over 70m long - the longest in Ireland. The cairn is aligned east-west across the edge of a natural shelf in the slope. The court opens at the east end, while the west end tapers to a fine point. The court is complete and provided access to the gallery through two well-matched entrance jambs. The gallery itself is full of cairn material having lost the upper part of its roof. The edges of the massive corbelling stones that supported the roof are visible poking through the top of the cairn.

Roughly halfway along the cairn there is a very interesting subsidiary chamber that has the structural plan of a portal tomb: if this was a lone, free-standing monument it would certainly be classified as a portal tomb. This structure has two large portal stones that flank a low doorstone. The chamber is quite small, but empty. Two large stones lie next to the chamber, one of which looks like it may have been a lintel that spanned the chamber, while the other is a massive gabled stone that must have looked very impressive when it was in place.

Moving back towards Ballymena to the foot of the Braid Valley there is a court tomb in **Ballymarlagh** TD. This is a monument that has suffered because of measures taken to protect it. A small area has been fenced off around the site to stop cattle and sheep trampling across it. As with many sites thus protected, this has allowed small trees and brambles to take over and hide the site from view. These would normally be

Subsidiary chamber at Antananum court tomb.

kept in check by grazing animals. Some thought really does need to be given to this when trying to 'protect' a site. In 1993 the then landowner and a team of enthusiasts did clear the site with a view to making it accessible to the public,[44] but the site has not been kept clear since then. This makes it extremely difficult to see the structure of the tomb today. It has a single court leading into a gallery that is segmented into four chambers and a subsidiary chamber.

Ballymarlagh was excavated by O. Davies in 1946 and 1947. The cairn rests on a layer of red clay that had charcoal mixed in to it. Sherds from Neolithic pots and burnt and unburnt flint flakes were found on this layer. The court area contained a lot of pottery, charcoal, porcellanite axes, burnt bone, and flint flakes and tools. Davies believed this to indicate that the court had been used as a pyre area.[45]

There is a roadside standing stone in *Carncome* TD 6km south-east of *Ballymarlagh*. This stands over 2m tall and has been incorporated into a modern, brick garden wall. This, frankly, looks terrible and completely spoils the character of the stone. It would have been much more sympathetic to divert the wall around the back of the stone, placing it in a little alcove, instead of just building the wall up against either side of it.

In *Ballyalbaanagh* TD, 12km east of *Carncome* inside a rectangular enclosure known locally as *The Ri*, there is a little-known court tomb of great interest. Despite being quite ruined there is enough of the monument present to see that the kerb was not straight, but curved inwards before straightening parallel to the gallery. Several stones from the court remain and some of the *façade* stones are *in situ*, but the kerb on the south side has been destroyed. Several rocky outcrops that were probably the

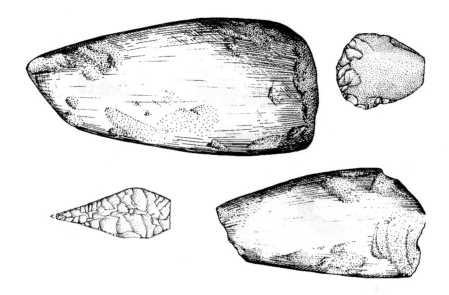

A selection of finds from Ballymarlagh (after Herity).

source of building material for the monument overlook the tomb. Nearby there is a barrow or small rath.

The Six Mile Water valley leads south-west inland from Larne. Overlooking the valley from opposite sides are two megalithic tombs. On the northern side is a small passage tomb known as *Carndoo* in **Ballyboley** TD, 4km east of **Ballyalbaanagh** and 6km south-west of Larne. This monument seems to have changed little since 1874, when Mr Kinahan wrote:

> The *kistvaen* was rudely built, and seemed to consist of eight stones, six standing, with two horizontal ones that rested on four of the others, the two standing-stones at the S. end forming a sort of doorway, but the N. end of the kistvaen was also open. A little to the N.E. of the kistvaen was a square standing stone, while to the E. of it was a large horizontal stone, said to cover bones.[46]

Borlase mentions that a stone, "having markings on it, described as a network of irregular rectilinear scorings"[47], was dug up in the field to the west of the tomb.

A small copse of thorn trees surrounds and hides the tomb today, although there is enough room in its centre to see the monument adequately. The structure is on a gentle slope, but it was built on a cairn-like structure that provides level platform for it. There are two stones from the east side of the court still in place. The outermost one of these is set into the edge of the cairn-platform so that it appears to cut through it. The 3m long gallery is still as described above and traces of ruined subsidiary cham-

Canders Walls from Borlase (1897).

bers can be seen throughout the copse. The front roofstone is a beautiful gabled stone, giving the entrance the appearance of a house with a pitched roof.

On the south side of Six Mile Water valley, in **Ballygowan** TD, are the sad remains of a once fine court tomb known as *Cander's Walls* (once known as *Caenorth's Wa's*). Today it is nothing more that a pile of very large slabs and boulders piled up against a fence, but the drawing in Borlase's *Dolmens of Ireland* depicts a wonderful structure. Approach to the site is via a farm lane that actually cuts through the rear of the tomb's cairn and it is possible to see a cross-section of it in the bank. On the opposite side of the track to the pile of stones there is a small set stone that may actually be the only stone from this monument that is still in its original location.

In 1940 the site was in a somewhat better state than it is today. The entry in the *Preliminary Survey of the Ancient Monuments of Northern Ireland* says that:

> … at least 4 uprights are in position and a cover slab (6ft. by 4ft.) is half fallen, while a dozen large slabs or boulders are thrown or built into fences. The remains defy description.[48]

Still in **Ballygowan** TD 2.5km south-west of *Cander's Walls*, there is a standing stone next to a lane. This is a beautifully shaped stone that tapers evenly to a point, making it look like a spearhead. A short distance from *Cander's Walls*, there used to be a ruined monument known locally as *The Druid's Altar*, which comprised of a standing stone and a large slab – presumably the capstone and one portal stone from a portal tomb. A recent investigation by the author found that there is no longer any local knowledge of the stones and that the site seems to have been destroyed.

Eight kilometres to the south of this standing stone, in **West Division** TD, there is a group of monuments. Two of these are relevant to this book – a stone row known as *The Three Brothers* and a cairn known as *The Schoolhouse Cairn*. The cairn is so named because a school was built on it, the foundations of which can still be seen today. *The*

Three Brothers are no longer standing. They lie in a row next to a farm track. It is not known if they originally stood where they now lie, or if they were moved to their current location. Either scenario is possible, as the lane may have been routed alongside the row or the stones could have been put to one side to allow the lane to cross the hill.

A little under 10km to the west of the stone row in **West Division** TD there is the famous holed standing stone at **Doagh** or **Holestone** TD. This standing stone is 1.5m tall with a hole pierced through it near to the top. Somewhat uninventively the stone is known as *The Hole Stone* and gives its name to the townland. The stone was used as a pledging stone, where couples would hold hands through the hole whilst getting married. A similar practice was observed at a stone on Inishcealtra, Co. Clare, where people would join hands through a hole in a stone called *The Bargaining Stone* whilst making pacts. *The Hole Stone* stands on the top of a flat-topped, 4m high rocky outcrop and is, unfortunately, surrounded by gorse bushes. This means that the stone is only visible from on top of the outcrop. When the bushes are cleared it can clearly be seen from below and its silhouette makes a fine picture. There are some rough rock-cut steps leading up one side of the outcrop to allow access.

A short distance to the west of *The Hole Stone* is a 'stone circle' known as *The Criags* in **Tobergill** TD. The reason why stone circle is in inverted commas is because although it appears on the OS map as a stone circle it is more likely to be the remains of a court tomb. Nearby there is an exposed rock face, which could be the quarry site from where the boulders were taken to build this monument. If this is the case, then this is a rare and special monument. Only one stone remains upright now. The other survivors lie in a semi-circle, which was probably the court of the tomb. Roughly at the centre of the arc of stones are several small stones that could, if it were a court tomb, be from the gallery.

To the north-west of *The Hole Stone* is **Browndod** court tomb and a standing stone known as *The Tardree Stone* which stands over 2m tall, also in **Browndod** TD. In the same townland there are other standing stones and another court tomb. At least two other megalithic tombs were recorded nearby that have since been destroyed.[49] The main court tomb at **Browndod** is an impressive one. Its gallery is segmented into four chambers and measures around 14m in length and its court is in good order, measuring 6m wide and deep. The trapezoidal cairn is also well defined and is an impressive 34m long. The only downside to this wonderful site is the electricity lines that run directly overhead. One of the supporting pylons is just 2m from the rear of the cairn, creating a weird juxtaposition of ancient and new, interesting and ugly. The site was excavated in May 1934 by E. Evans and O. Davies, revealing a red clay floor beneath the monument. Finds from the excavations included a mass of pottery sherds and a handful of flint implements. All the chambers had been plundered at some time, but traces of paving were found in one of the gallery chambers along with some charcoal. There were three pits in the court area that penetrated the bedrock.[50] The court area had a 'stone filling', similar to that found at **Ballymacaldrack** and **Ballyutuag**.

On the slopes below the court tomb mentioned above there is another, lesser-known court tomb in **Browndod** TD. This is visible from the road to the south of the hill. The remains are in poor condition in comparison to its neighbour, the gallery being all but destroyed. The court faces north into the hillside. The western side of the court is complete, represented by seven large orthostats, while just two stones represent the other side. Adjacent to the western arm of the court are two stones from the *façade*. There are two large recumbent stones at the head of the gallery that are probably the portal stones that framed its entrance.

Another of Co. Antrim's fascinating monuments is situated 5.5km south of **Browndod**: a cairn kerb in **Kilmakee** TD. This impressive circle of large green basalt stones is over 20m in diameter and contains forty-five stones. Each stone is over 1m tall and the cairn remains to the tops of the kerbstones. There is no sign of a central feature, but its scale does indicate that it was probably a passage tomb. The circumference of the circle has been planted with beech trees, the roots of which have gnarled their way over the kerbstones and seem to be gripping on to them.

In **Craigarogan** TD, 5.5km east-south-east of **Kilmakee**, is an impressive and unique passage tomb often referred to as *Carn Greine* or *Cairn Grainey*. As mentioned in the introduction, this monument has been the subject of writings for a very long time. In 1905 it was described in a write-up of an excursion of *The Royal Society of Antiquaries of Ireland* as:

> … [consisting] of about ten stones, raised on two upright rows, forming covering slabs, now much obscured by earth and stones gathered from agricultural opera-tions. It is about 40 feet long, the largest stone measuring 7 feet by about 5 feet and 2 feet thick. Formerly a circle of large stones surrounded it, but these are removed. Only one or two can be observed in an adjoining fence.[51]

In 1914 H.C. Lawlor carried out some excavations of the tomb, finding the burnt remains of several people and a cremated burial in an urn.

Craigarogan from Borlase (1897).

Over the last 100 years the monument has changed. The stones forming its structure are no longer 'obscured by earth and stones', but brambles are doing their best to replace them. The site is not visited as much as it should be, considering how special and unusual it is; as already stated, the tomb has no direct structural comparisons on the island. The northernmost chamber is not accessible from the rest of the monument, being blocked by a large septal slab that spans the monument. Similar features can be seen in some wedge tombs, such as Ballyedmonduff,[52] Co. Dublin, and Labbacallee,[53] Co. Cork. This sealed off chamber is covered by the largest of the monument's capstones. It is possible that this monument was built in two phases, with this chamber coming first or being a later addition. Removing this chamber from the site would leave a long gallery, which could be described as a simple wedge tomb. Removing the 'gallery' would leave a large megalithic kist, similar in plan and size to *The Dolmen of the Four Maols* at Ballina,[54] Co. Mayo.

Monument Types that Appear in this Book

Artificial Mounds

Across the country there are many manmade mounds that are not classified as barrows, mottes or passage tombs mainly because they have never been properly explored.

The vast majority of artificial mounds are round in plan and hemispherical in shape or truncated cones. These could be sod-covered cairns or simply piles of earth. Occasionally they are rectangular in plan with flat tops. Every one of them could be a burial monument, but some are likely to have been built as either viewing platforms or to mark the location of a long-forgotten event, such as a battle.

Until each site is individually researched their purpose will never be certain.

Barrows

Although barrows are not Neolithic, and certainly not megalithic in most cases, they are included here because their location can tell us a lot about habitation areas in the Neolithic and the period immediately following - the Bronze Age. In their most common form they consist of a raised earthen mound, which is often surrounded by a fosse (a ditch around a monument) and bank.

Unfortunately, the fact that barrows tended to be built near to habitation sites has its negative side too, because it means that they are often located on good quality land. This has led to many of them being ploughed away and they can be difficult to identify, especially from the ground. A great number of potential sites are identified from aerial photography through crop-marks, a distinctive change in the appearance of a crop when viewed from the air by the underlying monument altering soil conditions above it.

The area covered by a barrow can vary from as little as 5m to over 30m in diameter, but the average is in the region of 10-15m. Due to erosion and damage caused by ploughing it is difficult to define a typical height for barrows, but some of the better-preserved large examples approach 3m tall.

Burial rite is usually a single inhumation or a cremated burial. The burials are generally centrally placed, either in a pit or in a stone- or wood-lined chamber called a cist, which may or may not be covered by a capstone or wooden lid. Later, secondary burials are often found inserted into the covering mound.

One interesting contrast between megalithic monuments and barrows is that barrows often occur in groups or barrow cemeteries. Of the megalithic monuments only passage tombs share this trait.

There are several distinctive designs of barrow. Bell or Bowl barrows are the simplest type - a simple round mound. Some examples have a well-defined bank and ditch, usually referred to as a fosse, encircling them, whereas others have no fosse or bank. Long barrows are rare in Ireland and more common in England; they are elongated in plan with the burial(s) set towards one end. The earliest English examples, such as West Kennett, have megalithic chambers. Pond barrows are another rare style; they are indicated by a waterlogged depression surrounded by a bank and fosse and are not at all common in Ireland. Ring barrows are more like mini henges; they have no mound, but consist of a flat circular area demarked by a bank and fosse. Many of the barrows in Co. Antrim are of this type.

Passage Tombs

Passage tombs are so called because the burial chamber is reached via a passage leading from the outer edge of the covering mound or cairn. The walls of the passage, like those of the chamber, are usually constructed from large slabs standing up on end known as orthostats, but can be of dry-stone walling. The roof of the passage is constructed by placing large slabs on the tops of the orthostats. The chamber roof can be either made from similar horizontally laid slabs or by a method called corbelling. Corbelling is the process of placing successive layers of stones on top of each other, decreasing the gap with each layer to reduce the span until only a small opening remains. A single stone is placed across the space left at the top to form the last part of the roof. The chamber in Newgrange has one of the finest examples of a corbelled roof. A cruder version of a corbelled roof can be seen at *Carnanmore*, where a small number of massive slabs have been used to form a domed roof in a fashion more akin to the manner in which the roofs of court tombs were constructed.

The internal chambers of passage tombs vary in design. The 'classic' style is the cruciform chamber, where the main chamber has three sub-chambers leading off it, one opposite the passage and one off either side, forming a cross when viewed from above. In others the chamber is little more than a slight widening of the passage. Such examples are called undifferentiated passage tombs. The famous tomb at Newgrange has one of the finest cruciform chambers and Ireland's largest example, Knowth, has both a cruciform and an undifferentiated chamber. All of the examples in Co. Antrim are very simple, with single chambers. The large passage tomb at *West Toor*, for example, has an undifferentiated chamber, while the group around White Park Bay have small oval chambers.

Co. Antrim's passage tombs are very simple in design. They are all relatively small with a short passage leading to a box-like chamber in most cases. The only decoration found in Antrim's passage tombs is at *Carnanmore*, where a faded design can be found on one lintel (on a good day with good light).

Portal Tombs

Whereas passage tombs often occupy the most dramatic locations, portal tombs are, more often than not, situated in more subtle places such as in valleys or at the base of hills. This does not mean, however, that they are not spectacular in their own right, because the general characteristics of the class make them the most visually striking of all the tombs. These are the monuments that are usually referred to as Dolmens or Cromlechs.

Portal tombs are often grouped together with wedge and court tombs in the larger group of 'gallery tombs', but the chambers of portal tombs are never sub-divided by jambs or sill stones. A sill stone is a low stone set across the width of an opening and a jamb is a tall stone set against the wall of the chamber opposite another, leaving a space between them.

Whilst the many similarities between the different styles must be considered, this is, in the author's opinion, enough to warrant portal tombs being placed in a class of their own. The main argument is that the portal stones derive from the entrance jambs of court tombs and a small number of portal tombs show some signs of having a degenerate court such as can be seen at **Ticloy**. Such monuments, with small *façades/courts* and smaller chambers to the rear, could be the missing link between court tombs and portal tombs.[55] The embedded portal tomb in the cairn of the court tomb at **Antynanum** also provides a link. These two monuments are in the same valley and may have been built by the same people and even in use simultaneously.

The single chamber is usually formed with just three walls: a single slab forms the rear (the backstone) and in most cases single stones form the two sides of this box-like construction. Set in front of each of the sides is a taller stone, which projects forward occasionally inline with them, but they are more usually set just outside the side stones. Together these form an entrance or a 'portal' and are referred to as portal stones. Between these there is often an inset door stone, which occupies the full width of the portal and forms an alcove. The height of these door stones varies and can be half-, three-quarter- or full-height.

The structure is finished off with the capstone, usually a huge slab or block of stone that forms a roof. One end of this rests on the backstone with the other end resting on the portal stones. The front of the capstone projects forward beyond the portal stones creating a very dramatic and imposing monument when viewed in profile.

It does not seem to be the case that portal tombs were necessarily incorporated in a mound or cairn, but in many cases some evidence of some form of cairn survives. In such cases the monument is placed towards or at one end of a long sub-rectangular cairn. In no surviving instance does the cairn cover the capstone and many believe, including this author, that portal tombs were never intended to be entirely covered. Given their visually imposing form, this is more than likely. It would appear that the capstones were meant to be left exposed and that the cairn, when present, only served to hide the outside of the chamber walls.

Two of the portal tombs in **Ballyvennaght** TD are incorporated into the same cairn, with one occupying each end of it. This, although not common, does occur else-

Ticloy portal tomb

Plan of Ticloy (after Evans).

where with good examples being at Ballyrenan, Co. Tyrone, and Dyffryn Ardudwy, Merioneth, Wales.[56] A more extreme version can be found at Malin More, Co. Donegal where two portal tombs stand 90m apart with four smaller tombs in between them. All six of these may once have been incorporated into a single cairn.[57]

Standing Stones

What could be a more descriptive name? Also known as menhirs or monoliths, standing stones are structurally the simplest form of megalithic monument and the most common. They are quite simply stones that have been stood up intentionally by man, with one end set into the ground. However, their original purpose is far from straightforward for they have been erected during many time periods and for many different reasons.

Some were originally boundary markers, others such as the huge Punchestown standing stone (Co. Kildare) were erected to mark burials, while others marked locations significant to the Ancients and, just to add to the confusion, many were erected in modern times as scratching posts for cattle. Sometimes standing stones are found in association with stone circles. These are known as outliers.

Despite having such a basic form (what can be more basic than a single stone?) standing stones come in a massive variety of shapes and sizes and are the most varied of the monuments. At one extreme you have giant, phallic examples such as the Punchestown or Forenaghts Great standing stones (both in Co. Kildare) and at the other you have small, stumpy ones such as Knockiernan Lower (Co. Wicklow). Regardless of a stone's size or shape it is often possible to identify why that particular stone was selected. The Glencullen standing stone in Co. Dublin, for instance, is a beautiful cuboid block of solid quartz. Quartz plays a smaller, less 'in your face' role in many standing stones that have thin bands or veins of quartz running through them creating the impression of living rock complete with veins.

On the whole, the standing stones of Antrim fall into two categories: either quite small, such as the one in **Goakstown** TD or very big like the 2m plus giant at **Ballylig**.

Stone Rows and Stone Pairs

When standing stones are grouped together in a straight line, they become a stone row or an alignment. Two parallel stone rows form an avenue. Stone rows can be very short with just two stones or much longer - up to seven stones is quite common in Ireland. Some have even more. As with single standing stones the shape and size of the stones forming a row can vary greatly, even within a particular stone row. In Cork, for example, it is common for the stones to rise in height from one end to the other.

Occasionally the stones that occur in pairs are separated from the main group of stone rows and referred to as stone pairs. These can often be interpreted as being a male/female pairings because one stone is more slender and phallic in appearance than the other, which is usually more blunt and rounded.

Wedge Tombs

Wedge tombs have a sub-rectangular gallery divided into sub-chambers by low, full-width stones called sill stones or by two full-height stones set opposing each other known as jambs, leaving a narrow gap in between. This latter form is less common and shows a connection with court tombs.

They are called wedge tombs because of their distinctive shape. The front of the monument, which generally faces in a westerly direction, is both wider and taller than its rear.

A single stone spanning the entire width usually blocks the entrance. Two apparently localised trends differ from this rule. The wedge tombs of Co. Clare tend to have two stones blocking the entrance and those in Northern Ireland, for instance that at **Duntiege**, often have a single narrow stone centrally placed, which splits the entrance into two halves.

Some, such as Labacallee (Co. Cork) and Ballyedmonduff (Co. Dublin), have a sealed off sub-chamber built onto the rear of the gallery. Other, more common, architectural features also occur, called antechambers and porticos. These are both constructs attached to the front of the gallery, which are basically external sub-chambers. The main difference is that porticos are not closed at the front and are sometimes split in two by a vertical orthostat set along the central axis of the gallery.

The majority of wedge tombs were originally incorporated into a mound or cairn. The more simple structures were usually set into the centre of a round cairn, whereas the monuments with porticos etc. were often built into a D-shaped mound with the front of the gallery occupying a central position on the flat face. These D-shaped mounds can be quite exaggerated, giving more of a U-shape. It is quite common for the mound to have a small kerb. In a few rare instances more than one gallery was incorporated into a single mound. When this does occur the galleries are always parallel to one another and have their entrances facing in the same direction.

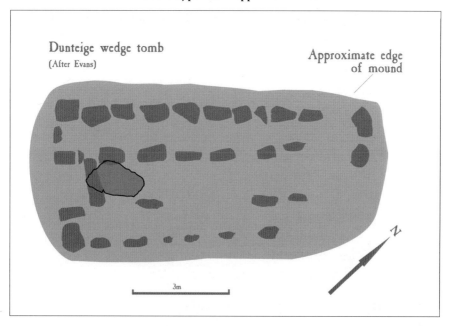

Dunteige wedge tomb
(After Evans)

Approximate edge
of mound

3m

Plan of Dunteige wedge tomb (after Evans) wedge.

Another question that must be addressed concerns the true role of these structures in the society of their builders. Their portrayal as communal burial places is contradicted by the lack of remains found in the few examples to have been investigated to date. Wedge tombs were built with sealed galleries, whereas the majority of court tombs, portal tombs and passage tombs are constructed to allow repeated access. This would indicate that wedge tombs were final resting places, but perhaps the other types were built as 'mortuary houses', where remains were only placed inside for a short period of time before being removed for disposal elsewhere at a yearly ceremony, for instance. This would certainly help explain the apparent lack of remains found at some sites.

Wedge tombs are by far the most numerous of the 'sepulchral' monuments in Ireland and, unlike all the other megalithic tombs, have a nationwide distribution. They are nearly always located to provide extensive views, usually to the west, but they rarely occupy the highest point in an area.

Gazetteer Introduction

The gazetteer is organised alphabetically by townland, which to some might be a little confusing as some of these sites are known by other names such as *Dooey's Cairn*, a court tomb in **Ballymacaldrack**. Townlands are used as the primary index because this is how Irish monuments are catalogued in the archaeological inventories. If this practice was more widely used, then cross-referencing sites would be far easier between resources. Where they exist, the common names for monuments are included in the indexes and mentioned in the text.

The author has visited all the sites included, but it should be borne in mind that most of these sites, although under state protection, are on private property and permission to visit should always be sought unless they are clearly signposted.

Most types of megalithic monument are present in Co. Antrim. Accompanying each description is the information needed to find the site. For most, directions will be given from the nearest town or landmark, the exceptions being where the directions are simply crazy due to the number of small roads involved. These directions will get you to the monument, but their presence here does not necessarily mean that there is a right of way. All of the entries will have the grid reference and the ordnance survey map(s) on which the sites can be found. The shape of the north Antrim coast means that the Ordnance Survey maps covering the county overlap slightly, so it is possible for monuments to appear on two maps. Where this is the case both sheets will be listed in the site's entry.

Except for the major places, it is recommend that the Ordnance Survey maps are used when planning journeys and for the final approach, but a small word of warning – at the time of writing, the road system of Ireland is undergoing so many alterations that often maps become out of date very quickly.

Co. Antrim is covered by eight Ordnance Survey (OS) maps, but only seven of them feature monuments in this book. These are from the Discoverer Series, published by Ordnance Survey Northern Ireland (OSNI). Northern Irish maps differ from the Discovery Series, produced by Ordnance Survey Ireland (OSI), that cover the Republic of Ireland, in several ways. The colours used to differentiate contour heights are more garish and ancient monuments are not marked with the convenient red dot, making them harder to locate on the OSNI maps.

Notes About Visiting Sites

Most of the monuments in this book are on private land and, no matter how you feel about property being theft and all that, you must respect this when visiting a site. Any damage or nuisance you caused could jeopardise the chances of other people being able to visit.

Always get permission to visit a site if necessary.

When on farmland, take care not to disturb livestock or damage crops.

Leave gates as you find them. If they are shut, shut them after you have passed through. If they are open, leave them open.

Always use paths where available and always walk around the edge of crop fields.

Never leave litter behind. THIS INCLUDES TEALIGHTS, CANDLES AND 'OFFERINGS' TO YOUR GODS OF CHOICE. People who visit after you do not want to be confronted with rotting flowers and wax covered stones. Hot wax is not just unsightly it also kills the lichen that has taken many, many years to grow.

Take any litter you come across away with you and dispose of it properly. I have returned from some trips with a black bag full of other people's rubbish.

Do not light fires in or near to monuments, you may be destroying unexcavated evidence just below the surface and the resultant black burnt patches are very unsightly for those that follow you.

Do not remove anything (except for litter) from a site.

Do not chalk in rock art to make it clearer. Take a bottle of water and pour it over the carvings. The reflections will make it just as clear as chalk does and no damage is done to the stones.

Have a thought for others who may be present. You might enjoy loud music while at the stones, but those around you may not.

Enjoy yourself.

One rule sums up all of the above (and more) very nicely:

LEAVE ONLY FOOTPRINTS

AND

TAKE ONLY MEMORIES

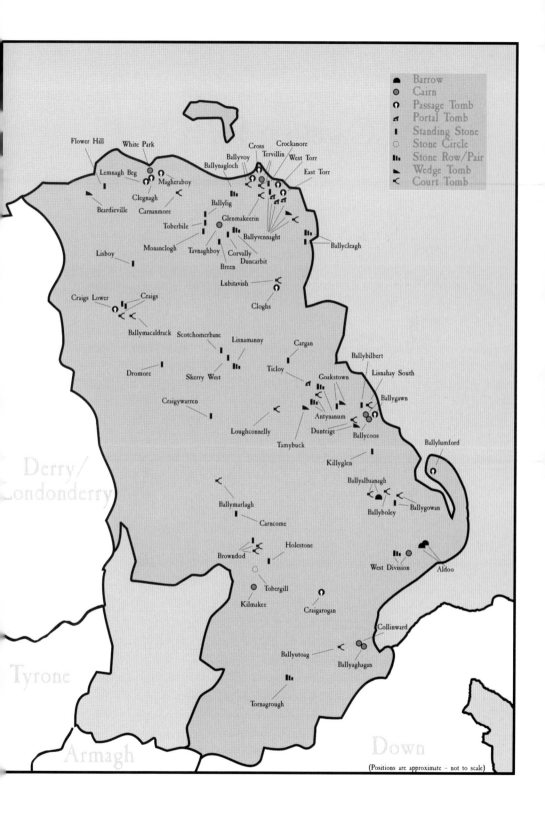

Barrow
Cairn
Passage Tomb
Portal Tomb
Standing Stone
Stone Circle
Stone Row/Pair
Wedge Tomb
Court Tomb

Flower Hill
White Park
Cross
Crockanore
Ballyvoy
Tervillin
West Torr
Ballynagloch
East Torr
Lemnagh Beg
Magheraboy
Clegnagh
Beardieville
Carnanmore
Ballylig
Toberbile
Glenmakeerin
Ballyvennaght
Monanclogh
Tavnaghboy
Corvally
Ballycleagh
Breen
Duncarbit
Lisboy
Lubitavish
Cloghs
Craigs Lower
Craigs
Ballymacaldrack
Scotchomerbane
Lisnamanny
Cargan
Ballybilbert
Dromore
Ticloy
Lisnahay South
Skerry West
Goakstown
Ballygawn
Craigywarren
Antynanum
Loughconnelly
Dunteige
Ballycoos
Tamybuck
Ballylumford
Killyglen
Ballyalbaanagh
Ballymarlagh
Carncome
Ballyboley
Ballygowan
Holestone
Browndod
West Division
Aldoo
Tobergill
Kilmakee
Craigarogan
Collinward
Ballyutoag
Ballyaghagan
Tornagrough

Derry/
Londonderry

Tyrone

Armagh

Down

(Positions are approximate – not to scale)

Gazetteer Index I

Monument Type Index

Passage Tombs

Portal Tombs

Gazetteer

Aldoo 1
Artificial Mound/Barrow
Grid Ref: J 376 900 (Sheet 15)

Directions: *From Carrickfergus take the B58 north-west towards Ballynure. The mounds are 2km past the B90 on the right, opposite a farmhouse.*

This impressive mound is located on the slopes of a shallow valley. At the head of the valley is a modern reservoir and the dammed stream that once flowed down the valley is now contained within a concrete watercourse.

 The grass-covered mound is 3m tall and at least 20m in diameter. There is some erosion on the southern side, probably caused by a combination of the weather and the tramplings of sheep. You shouldn't be too hard on the sheep, though, as the mound's preservation is probably due to the local tendency towards sheep farming, which has meant that this mound and its neighbour have not succumbed to the plough.

Mini-Gazetteer – 3km WSW there is a cairn at **West Division** known as the Schoolhouse Cairn. 5.8km NNW there is a standing stone at **Ballygowan**. 11.6km NW there is a court tomb at **Ballyalbaanagh**. 12.8km NNE there is a passage tomb st **Ballylumford**.

Aldoo 2
Artificial Mound/Barrow
Grid Ref: J 375 900 (Sheet 15)

Directions: *From Carrickfergus take the B58 north-west towards Ballynure. The mounds are 2km past the B90 on the right, opposite a farmhouse.*

This mound is just 100m to the west of the one mentioned above and is similar in every respect. This one is a little more difficult to see than the other as the slope above it and a large thorn hedgerow conspire to hide it from the road above.

Mini-Gazetteer – (see previous site)

Aldoo mound 1 from the east.

Aldoo mound 2 from the north-east.

Looking down into the court at Antynanum.

Antynanum or Antananum
Court Tomb
Grid Ref: D 256 110 (Sheet 9)

Directions: *From Carnlough head south-east on the A42 towards Ballymena. Turn right onto the B97 to Glenarm. After 1.5km you will pass a gate on the left-hand side of the road with 'Antananum' inscribed on one of the posts. Turn up the farm track opposite and continue to the last house and ask for directions to 'The Giant's Grave'.*

The OS maps show this busy townland as being *Antynanum*, but locally it can be seen written *Antananum*. Surprisingly, this massive court tomb is not marked on the OS maps, probably because it was omitted from the *Preliminary Survey of the Ancient Monuments of Northern Ireland* and has consequently 'fallen off the radar'. Consequently it is rarely visited (except by locals and academics) which is a shame, because the land-owner is very welcoming and, at 70m in length, the cairn is the longest court tomb cairn in Ireland.

The cairn is aligned roughly east-west with the court and gallery at the east end facing slightly north of east. The court is well-defined and in good condition with seven stones on the north side and six on the south. One of the stones on the north arm of the court has a deep solution pit on its inner face: a similar feature can be seen on the north entrance jamb of the court tomb at Carnagat, Co. Tyrone. Two large jambs lead into the 8m long gallery, which is full of cairn rubble. It appears that only the uppermost roofstones were removed when the gallery was opened, because the slanted corbel stones that would have supported them are still visible. At the gallery end of the cairn it stands an impressive 3m high. Along the south side of the cairn there is a wall of stones, which could be part of the original revetment that helped retain the cairn material. Along the rest of the cairn there has been slippage, which has hidden any traces of a kerb elsewhere.

The cairn tapers back to a fine low point interrupted in two places: once where a narrow path has been cut across it and also by the wonderful subsidiary chamber that stands roughly halfway along its length. This chamber should really be classed as 'an incorporated portal tomb' or similar. Certainly, if it were free standing, it would be classed as a portal tomb. This chamber is constructed with two 1.5m tall portal stones with a low doorstone between them. The chamber is formed from two pairs of sidestones and a backstone. Lying next to the chamber there are two large slabs that would have formed part of the roof, while tipped on one side next to the chamber there is a massive gable-shaped stone that probably sat on top of the other roof stones and rested on the portal stones. The entrance to this chamber is set back halfway into the cairn rather than being set on the cairn's edge as is more usual. This raises the question of which came first – was the subsidiary chamber added to the cairn at a later date or was the court tomb built to incorporate an existing portal tomb?

Some 500m to the west of the monument there is a long, low hill that shares the same alignment as the cairn. It is shaped like a long-cairn (i.e. rising steeply at one end and then tapering slowly to a point) and may have been the inspiration for position-ing this site where it is – i.e. to echo the hill.

Mini-Gazetteer – 550m WNW there is a stone pair in the same TD. 6km E there is a wedge tomb at **Goakstown**. 8.4km ESE there is a cairn at **Ballycoos**. 12.9km WNW there is a stone pair at **Lisnamanny**.

Antananum/Antynanum – The Maidens
Stone Pair
Grid Ref: D 260 104 (Sheet 9)

Directions: *From Carnlough take the A42 south-east towards Broughshane. 2km after pass-ing the junction with the B97 the A42 turns right at a crossroads – turn left here and continue for 3.5km, where there is a farm track on the left. Park here and walk along the track for 200m to a gate on the right. The stones are in the field through this gate.*

Unusually, this stone pair stands in a dip giving the site very limited views. The ground around them is very boggy and the tall reeds in the area make the stones difficult to see until you are close by.

Both stones are just over 1m tall and stand 3m apart on a rough north-south align-ment. The southern stone is quite slender, while the other is a wide slab-like stone

The Maidens at Antynanum.

making them a male/female pair. The thinner stone is very rough, while the larger stone is quite smooth in comparison with its northern edge nicely curved so that it looks like a half-buried D.

Mini-Gazetteer – 1.4km NNW there is a wedge tomb at **Tamybuck**. 6.7km ESE there is a wedge tomb at **Duntiege**. 8.1km E there is a court tomb at **Lisnahay South**. 14.7km SW there is a court tomb at **Ballymarlagh**.

Ballyaghagan
Cairn
Grid Ref: J 323 797 (Sheet 15)

Directions: *Park at the Cave Hill Country Park car park on the B95 near to the landfill. Walk to McArt's Fort. Once at the fort walk north-east to the highest point of the hill to find the cairn.*

The top of this 10m diameter cairn has been removed exposing a small cist at its centre. Only the tops of the numerous stones forming this chamber are visible, because it has been filled in with other stones from the cairn, either for its protection or the safety of the many walkers that cross the cairn.

Ballyaghagan cairn from the east.

The flat top of the levelled cairn is just 1m high and often used as a convenient launch platform by kite-flyers.

Mini-Gazetteer – 3.3km W there is a court tomb at *Ballyutoag*. 6.8km NW there is a passage tomb at *Craigarogan*. 11.5km NNE there are two artificial mounds at *Aldoo*. 12.2km ESE there is a standing stone at *Ballybeen*.

Ballyalbaanagh
Barrow
Grid Ref: J 289 974 (Sheet 9)

Directions: *Follow the directions to the court tomb below and walk south to find this.*

This site, known locally as *The Fort*, could either be a ring barrow or a very small rath. It is 10m in diameter and its outer bank is no more than 50cm high. There is a silted up ditch within the outer bank and a small depression at the centre of the monument could be where treasure hunters have investigated the site. The site is mentioned here mainly due to its proximity to the wonderful court tomb in this townland.

Mini-Gazetteer – see next site.

Ballyalbaanagh rath/barrow.

Ballyalbaanagh
Court Tomb
Grid Ref: J 288 975 (Sheet 9)

Directions: *From Kells follow the B53 north-east and join the A36 east towards Larne. Turn right onto the B94 and head south for 5km and turn left. Go straight on at the first crossroads and continue for a little over 1km. Turn left up the second farm track and drive up to the farm, keeping to the right at any junctions. Ask at the farm for directions to The Ri.*

This court tomb is situated in one corner of a rectangular, dry-stone built enclosure known locally as *The Ri*. The quadrant that the tomb occupies has been separated from the rest of the compound by an internal dry-stone wall. Just outside the enclosure to the north there are some exposed rocky outcrops, which were probably the quarry site for the monument's stones. The tomb is not marked on the Ordnance Survey map, but the outcrops are.

The tomb's east-west aligned gallery is in poor condition and the kerb on the south side has been robbed away. The kerb on the north side is in extremely good condition, though, and is of a very interesting design. From the widest point of the *façade* the kerb curves back and angles in towards the gallery. 1m from the gallery it straightens up and then runs parallel with it. This gives the monument a wine glass shape when viewed from above.

The site slopes to the south slightly and to deal with this the builders seem to have

Ballyalbaanagh court tomb from the east.

chosen taller stones for the south side of the court than for the north side rather than levelling the ground.

The east-facing court is in bad condition, too, but there are enough stones remaining to give a good impression of its dimensions. Leading off the northern arm of the court are two stones forming the narrow *façade* on that side. One stone on the south side of the court may also be part of the *façade*.

Discovering this rarely visited site for the first time is a wonderful experience. It may be ruinous, but its location and rarity of design make it quite special.

Mini-Gazetteer – 4km E there is a court tomb known as *Carndoo* at **Ballyboley**. 8.2km SW there is a holed standing stone at **Holestone**. 9.7km WSW there is a court tomb at **Browndod**. 10.6km SW there is a 'stone circle' at **Tobergill**.

Ballyboley - Carndoo
Court Tomb
Grid Ref: J 328 973 (Sheet 9)

Directions: *From Larne travel south-west along the A8 towards Belfast and turn right onto the A36 towards Ballymena. Turn left at the first crossroads and continue to another crossroads and turn right. 2km along this road you will pass a left-hand turn. Access to the site is via the farm 500m past this junction on the right.*

The entrance to Ballyboley court tomb.

Not many court tombs still have their roof, so this one is quite special. Only a 2m length of its gallery remains along with a small section of its court. The north–south aligned gallery opens to the south where two fine jambs form its entrance. The west side of the south-facing court is missing, but several stones from the east side remain. These rise in height as they progress away from the entrance.

Six orthostats from the gallery are in place. These are shorter than the entrance jambs by 40cm. The front roofstone is beautifully gabled and rests upon the orthostats behind the jambs, calling into question the post-restoration positioning of the similar shaped roofstone at Creggandevesky (Co. Tyrone), which sits on the entrance jambs. The second of the two roofstones is just a normal block of stone. The underside of the gabled roofstone is kept level by the insertion of a small 'chocking' stone between it and one of the orthostats that it rests on.

The tomb is built upon a 1m high platform of cairn material. The outermost court stone is set into the edge of this platform. The whole structure is hidden from view by a thicket of thorn trees that covers the raised area. Grazing sheep have kept the north side of this thicket quite clear, revealing the much-disturbed remains of a possible subsidiary chamber and the ruined rear of the gallery.

Mini-Gazetteer – 3.2km E there is a ruined court tomb known as *Cander's Walls* at **Ballygowen**. 7.1km N there is a standing stone at **Killyglen**. 8.6km S there is a stone row known as *The Three Brothers* at **West Division**. 12.4km N there is a passage tomb at **Ballygawn**.

Ballycleagh stone pair.

Ballycleagh
Stone Pair
Grid Ref: D 249 334 (Sheet 5)

Directions: *Head north from Cushendunon the B92. Just outside the town the road turns sharply left and a road heads off to the right. Follow the road to the left and turn into the caravan park shortly afterwards. The stone is in the main car park area.*

These two large stones stand over 5m apart in a field next to a track that leads to a house and cottage above a raised beach. They are aligned north-south.

The northernmost stone is the largest at 2m tall, while the other is just under 2m. A third stone that was once in a nearby hedge could have come from this monument making it a ruined stone row, not a stone pair.

Mini-Gazetteer – 5km NW there is a portal tomb at ***Ballyvennaght***. 6.7km SW there is a passage tomb at ***Cloghs***. 8km NNW there is a passage tomb at ***West Torr***. 10.2km W there is a stone pair at ***Duncarbit***.

Ballycleagh
Standing Stone
Grid Ref: D 246 332 (Sheet 5)

Directions: *Head north from Cushendunon the B92. Just outside the town the road turns sharply left and a road heads off to the right. Take this road and look out for the stones on the right-hand side after 500m.*

Ballycleagh
standing stone.

This 1.7m tall slab is now incorporated into a small garden feature at the entrance to Cushendun Caravan Park. It is slowly being consumed by clematis. It is hard to know whether this is the only slab-like standing stone in Co. Antrim or if it was originally part of a megalithic tomb.

Mini-Gazetteer – 4.4km WNW there is a wedge tomb at ***Ballyvennaght***. 6.3km NNW there is a passage tomb at ***East Torr***. 6.4km SW there is a passage tomb at ***Cloghs***. 12.3km NW there is a passage tomb at ***Ballyvoy***.

Ballycoos
Cairn
Grid Ref: D 332 074 (Sheet 9)

Directions: *From Larne take the A8 west and then head north along the B148. After 4.5km the road turns sharp right and a small road carries on ahead. Take this road and follow it for 4km until you reach a car park on the left and park. The cairn is on the opposite side of the road on a raised area.*

This 10m diameter site is marked as an enclosure on the OS map, but its form and position make it more likely to be a robbed out cairn. The centre of the cairn has been completely robbed away leaving just a raised edge around its circumference, thus the interpretation as an enclosure. It is situated on a low, steep-sided knoll that overlooks a mountain pass. The material that has been removed from the monument was probably used when the road below was laid.

The remains of Ballycoos cairn.

Mini-Gazetteer – 2.6km NNE there is a passage tomb at **Ballygawn**. 7.8km WNW there is a stone pair known as *The Maidens* at **Antynanum**. 10.9km WNW there is a portal tomb at **Ticloy**. 14.3km W there is a court tomb at **Loughconnelly**.

Ballygawn
Cairn
Grid Ref: D 338 090 (Sheet 9)

Directions: *From Larne take the A8 west and then head north along the B148. After 4.5km the road turns sharp right and a small road carries on ahead. Take this road and follow it for 4km until you reach a car park on the left and park. Follow the Ulster Way footpath to the second peak. Here you will find three 'peaks'. The rightmost one is the cairn.*

At first sight this low mound looks like the other lumps and bumps along the hilltop. However, the cairn material poking through the grass, a large stone at its centre and its almost perfectly circular circumference give its true form away.

The top of the cairn has been robbed away leaving a 1m high platform with stunning views to the east and along the coast. To the south-west Slemish Mountain can be seen.

Mini-Gazetteer – 1.6km WSW there is a court tomb at **Duntiege**. 2.8km NW there is a wedge tomb at **Goakstown**. 8.9km WNW there is a stone pair at **Antynanum**. 11.8km SE there is a passage tomb at **Ballylumford**.

Ballygawn cairn from the west.

Ballygawn passage tomb.

Ballygawn - Cloughogan
Passage Tomb
Grid Ref: D 345 096 (Sheet 9)

Directions: *From Larne head north along the A2 coast road to Ballygalley. In Ballygalley turn left to Carncastle. Once in Carncastle turn right and head north on the B 148. 2km north of Carncastle turn left up a farm track directly opposite a small cluster of houses and ask at the farm for directions.*

In the nineteenth century this monument served time as a chicken coup and pigsty. It is officially classified as a portal tomb, but it is more akin to the passage tomb at **Ballylumford**. Its single capstone is of similar proportions, as is the chamber. Another similarity is that the eastern orthostat is a large split boulder with the flat surface facing inwards.

The single chamber is 1.5m tall and 2m x 1m in plan. The whole structure is built into a turn in a thick dry-stone wall so that the entrance is accessible. The old farmhouse is just 2m from the monument.

In 1884 William Gray noted the following:

It forms part of a boundary hedge near a farm cottage, and has done service for many years as a pigsty and poultry-house. For this purpose, the open space between the uprights have been carefully filled in with small stones. The thrifty housewife who made this change claims the credit of having built the house; her worthy spouse, however, contends that the Danes built Cloughogan before the memory of man, and that the old woman only built the byre.[58]

Today there is little sign of the stones that once filled the gaps between the orthostats and the wall has collapsed into the back of the chamber partially filling it.

The site's wonderful history and unusual (but not unique) incorporation into a farmyard as a utilitarian building makes this a great monument to visit.

Mini-Gazetteer – 2.7km SW there is a wedge tomb at **Duntiege**. 5.4km S there is a standing stone at **Killyglen**. 11.5km W there is a portal tomb at **Ticloy**. 14.4km S there is a standing stone at **Ballygowan**.

Ballygilbert
Standing Stone
Grid Ref: D 334 104 (Sheet 9)

Directions: *From Larne head north along the A2 coast road to Ballygalley. In Ballygalley turn left to Carncastle. Once in Carncastle turn right and then take the next left. Follow this* *road to the Ulster Way car park. Park and cross over the road and follow the Ulster Way north-wards to find the stone. This is a 3km walk over 2 peaks.*

There are many standing stones that can be described as being phallic, but this is probably the most phallic of all.

This large stone is 1.6m tall, 1m thick at its base and round in plan. The shaft rises 1m before bulging out in a mushroom-like fashion before tapering to a point, giving the appearance of an enlarged *glans*.

It stands close to the eastern edge of a wide plateau atop Ballygilbert hill alongside the Ulster Way footpath. It is set far enough back from the edge to prevent it being seen from the thin piece of coastal land below, which is a little unusual. To the south-west low rising peaks on the hilltop block the view towards Slemish. A similar effect to the west hides Knoklayd Mountain. This is a site without either of the expected landmarks as reference points in its landscape, which adds to the feeling of unease when trying to assess its location.

Mini-Gazetteer – 800m ENE there is a court tomb at **Lisnahay South**. 3km S there is a cairn at **Ballycoos**. 7.8km W there is a court tomb at **Antynanum**. 13.7km SSW there is a court tomb at **Ballyalbaanagh**.

Ballygilbert standing stone: probably the most phallic standing stone in the world.

Ballygowan - Cander's Walls
Court Tomb
Grid Ref: J 360 969 (Sheet 9)

Directions: *From Larne head south-east along the A8 towards Belfast and turn right onto the B100. Turn right after 3.5km at the first crossroads. The tomb is accessed via the first track-way on the left-hand side. Ask at the house.*

Of all the cases of Antrim monuments destroyed in the last century this could be the greatest loss. Drawings from the nineteenth century depict an array of massive stones set in an arc with some others leaning against them, so it had obviously been partially destroyed even then. Today there is nothing more than a pile of large boulders and slabs at the edge of a field, one of which may still be set.

A farm track has been cut through the back of the monument exposing a cross-section through the tail end of the cairn. In the field on the opposite side of the track to the bulk of the remains there is a low, set stone that may be the only surviving stone still *in situ*. This is presumably a kerbstone.

Mini-Gazetteer – 3.2km W there is a court tomb known as *Carndoo* at **Ballyboley**. 7.1km SE there two artificial mounds at **Aldoo**. 11.7km NNW there is a wedge tomb at **Duntiege**. 13.7km N there is a standing stone at **Ballygilbert**.

The sad remains of Cander's Walls, Ballygowan.

Ballygowan standing stone.

Ballygowan
Standing Stone
Grid Ref: J 350 952 (Sheet 9)

Directions: *From Larne head south-east along the A8 towards Belfast and turn right onto the B100. Turn right after 3.5km at the first crossroads. Continue for 2.5km and turn left at the crossroads. The stone is at the top of the first lane on the right.*

When viewed from a slight angle this stone looks like a mighty spearhead erupting from the ground. When viewed head-on, however, it is very anthropomorphic, with two evenly sized shoulders either side of a round-topped 'head'. The fashioning of these shoulders seems to be deliberate.

The stone is 1.5m tall and occupies a site at the top of a field overlooking a farm-house. Large trees block the views in most directions.

Mini-Gazetteer – 2km NNE there is a court tomb in the same TD. 2.2km SE there is a standing stone at **Ballynarry**. 10.2km NE there is a passage tomb at **Ballylumford**. 13.6km SW there is a passage tomb at **Craigarogan**.

Ballylig standing stone.

Ballylig
Standing Stone
Grid Ref: D 091 380 (Sheet 5)

Directions: *From Bally castle take the A44 south towards Armoy. The road turns sharply left where it meets the B67. 1.5km after this bend take a left turn and then turn left up the first farm track. The stone is at the top of this lane on the left.*

At 2m tall this stones equals any of the other standing stones around Knocklayd Mountain and its gentle curving profile makes it the most attractive. This profile makes it look like a petrified wave, frozen as it made its way across the field.

The site is on the foot-slopes of the mountain affording it with excellent views across the county to the west. The rounded form of Knocklayd Mountain provides an excellent backdrop to the stone, but visit late in the day when the sun is to the west if you wish to capture this image.

It has been suggested that it may represent the remains of a portal tomb, but the presence of so many other large standing stones around this side of Knocklayd would indicate that this is just another example.

Mini-Gazetteer – 2.3km SSW there is a standing stone at ***Monanclogh***. 7.7km ENE there is a passage tomb at ***Ballyvoy***. 9.5km ENE there is a passage tomb at ***Cross***. 11.7km E there is a portal tomb at ***Ballyvennaght***.

Ballylumford
Passage Tomb
Grid Ref: D 430 016 (Sheet 9)

Directions: *From Carrickfergus follow the A2 east towards Whitehead. Continue along the A2 when it turns north for 1.5km and turn right onto the B150 towards Island Magee. Continue for 6.5km and take a left-hand turn signposted Ballylumford. Continue for 4km keeping an eye out for the tomb on the right-hand side of the road.*

If this wonderful monument were not situated near to the north end of Island Magee, a long peninsula with narrow roads, it would be one of the most visited sites in Ireland. This limitation must be of some relief to the landowners, because it is literally in their front yard, just 3m from their front door. It certainly beats having a garden gnome!

Now surrounded by slabs, gravel and a low chain, the four orthostats of the single chamber hold the 1.5m square roofstone 1.5m above the ground, giving the structure an elegant box-like appeal. The largest orthostat (the one nearest the front door) is a split boulder set with its flat face inwards. Within the chamber a small stone can be seen poking through the gravel, which may be a sillstone.

The extreme proximity of the house and the tall trees on the opposite side of the road block all the views that were once to be experienced from this location. A drawing from the early nineteenth century shows that it once enjoyed an open view to the

Ballylumford passage tomb.

north-east over Larne and to the mountains beyond.[59] Borlase mentions that in 1832 there were six stones surrounding the central chamber, but then confusingly continues that:'… and formerly there were six upright stones outside the monument to the N., and two to the S., measuring 3 feet in height.'[60]

As Borlase went on to comment, the presence of stones to the north and south of the monument indicates that a large kerb originally surrounded the site.

Mini-Gazetteer – 10km SW there is a standing stone at **Ballynarry**. 11.7km NW there is a passage tomb at **Ballygawn**. 12.8km SSW there are 2 artificial mounds at **Aldoo**. 14.7km NW there is a standing stone at **Goakstown**.

Ballymacaldrack – Dooey's Cairn
Court Tomb
Grid Ref: D 021 183 (Sheet 8)

Directions: *From Dunloy follow the B16 south and then follow the signs. This is not a long journey as the site is only 1.5km outside Dunloy.*

Access to this roadside monument is not as easy as it could be. Parking in the narrow road is limited and the kissing gates make disabled access almost impossible. As is so

The court of Dooey's Cairn, Ballymacaldrack.

often the case, not enough land around the site was purchased when it was made into a National Monument.

There is a single south-west-facing court, which is almost complete. This is not semicircular, but starts to close up, giving a more wineglass-shaped plan. The edges of the 20m long trapezoidal cairn are still visible, with kerbstones still in place along the northern and southern edges. The gallery is less well defined and today it appears as if many of the stones from the rear section are missing. This is not the case, however. The open area behind the gallery marks the location of a stone-lined, paved trench.

The excavations here in 1935 by Professor E. Eystyn Evans were amongst the earliest to be made of a court tomb. It was Evans who named the site *Dooey's Cairn* in honour of the landowner – Andrew Dooey – for 'much encouragement and practical help'. In documents and references from Professor Evans' time you will see the name spelled *Doey*, but the family now use *Dooey*[51]. It was the excavation of this monument that first led Evans to suggest a link between the newly recognised Irish court tomb and the tombs of the Clyde region of Scotland. The site was re-excavated again in 1975 by A. Collins to attempt to get a radiocarbon date for the site.

The findings of both excavations were remarkable, showing extended use of the monument for a period spanning at least 500 years. Three charcoal samples produced dates of 2990BC $\pm$ 50, 3200BC $\pm$ 90 and 2680 $\pm$ 130.[52] The later date came from material filling the court area, while the earlier date came from the stone-lined trench mentioned above, which appears to have been a cremation trench. This is one of the very rare examples of cremations being performed at the site of a monument.

The gaps between the orthostats forming the court were filled with horizontally laid stones, forming a solid wall holding back the cairn material. The visual effect of this form of walling can best be seen at the reconstructed court tomb at Annaghmare, Co. Armagh. Part of the gallery walling was formed with dry-stone techniques, which seemed an unusual choice given the abundance of stone in the immediate area. Collins remarked that if this was a repair, then it was done early in the tomb's cycle of use. The forecourt was cleared in the later excavation when pottery sherds, flint flakes and a flint core were found amongst the rubble that filled it. In 1935 several examples of worked flint, including three arrowheads, were uncovered.

Mini-Gazetteer – 4.3km W there is a court tomb at *Craigs*. 9.6km E there is a standing stone at *Scotchomerbane*. 13.3km W there is a passage tomb at Moneydig (Co. Derry). 14.5km SE there is a standing stone at *Craigywarren*.

Ballymarlagh
Court Tomb
Grid Ref: D 141 018 (Sheet 9)

No picture, as the site is too overgrown.

Directions: *Take the A36 east from Ballymena. Take the second left after passing the M2 junction (approx 1.5km). 500m along this lane you will reach a double gate on the right-hand side of the road. Looking up the field from the left-hand gate the thicket covering this monument can be seen next to the hedge.*

It is always disappointing when you see a monument that is obviously a good specimen and is being neglected. The cairn of this court tomb is covered with a thicket of thorn trees that makes it very difficult to make out what remains are hidden beneath. The 10m long segmented gallery could just be made out and one side of the court was just visible in 2002. The site was cleared by the landowner in the summer of 1993, but it has been left to its own devices ever since and the brambles grow thicker with each passing year.

Underneath all the vegetation there is a 30m long trapezoidal cairn. The long gallery is segmented into four chambers. The east-south-east-facing court is nearly a fully circular one and excavations in 1948 revealed that it contained a small cairn under which was a black layer containing flints and pottery sherds (see *Ballutoag*). Other finds from the site included flint arrowheads and two blue-stone polished axes from the Tievebulliagh axe factory.[53] Traces of dry-stone walling were found between the stones forming the court. Having lost this part of the structure many court tombs look too skeletal, almost naked, but remembering this commonly encountered feature helps the visitor to ruinous court tombs to visualise what the site would have looked like when first built. At the opposite end of the cairn to the court there is a single chamber with a 'sill-and-jambs'[54] entrance.

There is a fence around the site to protect it, with a collapsing style allowing entry. The extensive views to the west that could have once been enjoyed from this monument are now mainly blocked by nearby hedgerows.

Mini-Gazetteer – 6.3km SSE there is a standing stone at *Carncome*. 9km NNE there is a court tomb at *Loughconnelly*. 10.4km SSE there is a standing stone known as *The Tardree Stone* at *Browndod*. 13.3km NE there is a wedge tomb at *Tamybuck*.

The taller of the stones at Ballynaglogh.

Ballynaclogh/Ballynaglogh
Stone Pair
Grid Ref: D 148 408 (Sheet 5)

Directions: *From Ballycastle head east on the A2. The church with stones is 2km outside of town on the left-hand side of the road.*

The reuse of ancient sites for more recent religious activity is a common one, but it is rare to find such a modern church built next to a megalithic monument. These two stones now stand in the graveyard of the modern Church of Ireland Culfeightrin church. The shortest stone is located close to the south-east corner of the church and appears to have been broken. The tallest stone stands 3m high, just outside the entrance to the church, welcoming people to and from services.

There are two other stones in the graveyard that may be associated with the two that stand, making it a stone row rather than a stone pair. One of these is large boulder, while the other is more like a standing stone, which lies near to the east end of the church.

The shorter of the two main stones is now amongst the modern graves, which is quite fitting, because two cist burials where supposedly found near to it. The presence of multiple standing stones and cist burials makes this an interesting site.

Unfortunately, the modern activity around the site makes it impossible to investigate the area properly.

Mini-Gazetteer – 1.4km NE there is a passage tomb at **Ballyvoy**. 3.4km ENE there is a cairn at **Tervillin**. 4.2km ENE there is a standing stone at **Crockanore**. 7.3km WSW there is a standing stone at **Toberbile**.

Ballyutoag – Hanging Thorn Cairn
Court Tomb
Grid Ref: J 290 794 (Sheet 15)

Directions: *From west Belfast take the A52 towards Crumlin. Just outside the city there is a hairpin bend followed by a turnoff to the B95. Continue along the A52 for 2km and turn left at the first crossroads. The tomb is 1km along this road on the left-hand side. Ask at the farm to the south.*

This ruined court tomb was built on a south-east-facing slope along a north-south alignment. The gallery has all but disappeared with one or two very low stones from its structure remaining. In contrast the 5m diameter court is in very good condition with eleven of its stones remaining. Most of these are quite low, but both arms have

The court of Ballyutoag court tomb.

large stones halfway along their length. The entrance jambs are different shapes and separated by a 40cm long sill stone.

The court area is blocked off by a wall that runs up the hill and across the front of it. During excavation in 1937 by I.J. Herring the court was found to contain a small cairn,[55] traces of which can still be felt underfoot. Charcoal from the court area was dated to 4120 ± 200 BP[56]. The site was given the name *Hanging Thorn Cairn* by Herring during excavations[57], presumably because of the thorn trees that overhang the court.

Mini-Gazetteer – 5.1km NNW there is a passage tomb at **Craigarogan**. 6.4km SW there is a stone pair on *Standing Stones Hill* at **Tornagrough**. 11.3km NNE there is a cairn at **West Division**. 12.3km SSE there is a henge, passage tomb and standing stone at Ballynahatty (Co. Down).

Ballyvennaght
Court Tomb
Grid Ref: D 209 355 (Sheet 5)

Directions: *This site requires a GPS and Ordnance Survey Map to locate.*

This is a difficult monument to find. There is no cairn material visible and the short gallery is ruined, but partially covered by a capstone. The remaining stones of the court indicate that it took the form of a shallow V facing south. The ground to the north rises steeply above the tomb forcing all views to the south.

Ballyvennaght is a large townland with several monuments. This tomb and the nearby wedge tomb are located away from the concentration of portal tombs, which are just over 1km to the north of them.

Mini-Gazetteer – (see *Cloughananca* below)

Ballyvennaght 1
Portal Tomb
Grid Ref: D 207 365 (Sheet 5)

Directions: *This site requires an OS Map and compass/GPS to locate*

The top layer of peat around this monument has been removed exposing the capstone, the tops of the portal stones and the tops of the chamber orthostats. The chamber has been dug out, but is usually filled with water. Around the base of the capstone remains of the cairn can be seen.

The remains of Ballyvennaght court tomb.

Ballyvennaght 1 portal tomb.

The chamber is a small, narrow one measuring about 1.8m x 60cm in plan. It is not possible to tell exactly how tall the structure would be if fully excavated from the peat. The capstone is still *in situ* and measures 2m long and just over 1m wide.

In a direct line extended backwards along the axis of the tomb there is a large boulder embedded in the peat. This gives the impression that there may be a second tomb here as there is at the main **Ballyvennaght 3** portal tomb site, but this is doubtful.

Mini-Gazetteer – (see **Cloughananca** below)

Ballyvennaght 2
Portal Tomb
Grid Ref: D 209 366 (Sheet 5)

Directions: *This site requires an OS Map and compass/GPS to locate.*

This collapsed portal tomb is the worst of the three examples found in this townland. The long capstone lies at ground level, slightly displaced from the orthostats below. The orthostats are heavily buried and the chamber has not been emptied, making this a very disappointing monument to visit.

Mini-Gazetteer – (see **Cloughananca** below)

Ballyvennaght 3 - Cloughananca
Portal Tombs
Grid Ref: D 200 368 (Sheet 5)

Directions: *It is best approached from a gate alongside the A42 at D 203 362. To reach this gate, follow the A2 south-east from Ballycastle through Ballypatrick Forest. 1.5km after passing the entrance to Ballycastle Forest on the left the road curves gently left and then right as it leaves the forest. The gate is on the left on this bend. Parking is possible, but tricky. From the gate follow the edge of the forest until you reach a square fenced compound. Walk around this to the right – DO NOT walk between it and the forest as there is a very deep boggy hole there. Once past the compound you will be able to see the top of the capstone poking up above the heather and grasses. This whole area is very boggy, so caution is needed.*

This is an example of a rare double portal tomb. Others can be found at Ballyrenan (Co. Tyrone) and Toome (Co. Donegal). Early descriptions of **Ticloy** portal tomb indicate that may have been a double portal tomb, too.

These two portal tombs are built 60m apart at opposite ends of a long, low, east-west aligned cairn that is 2m below the level of the peat around the site. A deep trench has been dug out to the level of the cairn material to reveal both monuments.

The eastern tomb has collapsed under the weight of the massive capstone, which now lies on top of the fallen orthostats. The other monument is still upright and nearly complete – just one side stone from the chamber is missing. The capstone is 4m x 3m and over 1m thick.

A half-height doorstone stands between the 1.8m tall portal stones of the western monument. Both portal stones lean to the north slightly with the southern leaning slightly more than the other, giving the capstone a peculiar angle when viewed from the front. This tomb faces west away from the cairn, but it does not necessarily follow that the eastern tomb faced outwards in the same way. Other double portal tombs such as Ballyrenan (Co. Tyrone) and Dyffryn Ardudwy (Gwynedd, North Wales) have both tombs facing in the same direction, i.e. one of them faces into the cairn.

The landscape around the **Ballyvennaght** portal tombs forms a natural amphitheatre and limits the views from these monuments. Not even Knocklayd Mountain to the west is visible due to the intervening hills.

Mini-Gazetteer –4km NNE there is a passage tomb at *West Torr*. 5.1km NNW there is a standing stone at *Crockanore*. 6.6km NW there is a stone pair at *Ballynaglogh*. 11.7km W there is a standing stone at *Monanclogh*.

The exposed capstone of Ballvennaght 2 portal tomb

Left: Cloghananca portal tombs at Ballyvennaght.

Below: The better of the two portal tombs at Ballyvennaght.

Ballyvennaght standing stone.

Ballyvennaght
Standing Stone
Grid Ref: (Sheet 5)

Directions: *Follow the directions for **Ballyvennaght 3** above. Once at the tombs continue walking north and you will soon see the stone ahead of you.*

There are not many standing stones that are placed in as picturesque a location as this one. It is a shame that it is so difficult to reach. It stands overlooking a deep gorge carved by a confluence of streams as they leave the boggy plateau to the south. The sound of the water below echoes up and has a very relaxing effect. It is easy to see why someone thought it worthwhile to mark this spot.

The stone is 1.8m tall and aligned north-south.

Mini-Gazetteer – (see *Cloughananca* above)

Ballyvennaght
Wedge Tomb
Grid Ref: (Sheet   )

Directions: *This site requires an OS Map and compass/GPS to locate. It is best approached from Loughareema.*

Looking north over the remains of Ballyvennaght wedge tomb.

Of all the monuments in the large townland of **Ballyvennaght** this is in the poorest condition. With so many other fine monuments close by it is a site for the completist only.

The remains are a total mess, with only a few stones remaining in position. There is some evidence of double walling and a few stones can be identified as probable roofstones.

Mini-Gazetteer – (see *Cloughananca* above)

Ballyvoy
Court Tomb
Grid Ref: D 158 417 (Sheet 5)

Directions: *Head east from Ballycastle along the A2 for 3.5km and turn left at the crossroads. Continue to the farm at the end of the lane and ask for permission and directions.*

Only the gallery and a small section of the kerb at its rear remain here. The tomb is built near to the top of a west-facing slope with a ridge of rock to its east rising up behind it to a round peak. There is a ruinous passage tomb at the top of the hill (see below).

Looking west over Ballyvoy court tomb.

The sides of the east-west aligned gallery are constructed from huge slabs set in evenly matched pairs apart from at the rear. At this point the two opposing stones could not be more different: one is low and slender, while the other is very large. The rear of the gallery is terminated with a low, gabled stone. A line of stones of unknown purpose extends southwards from the rear of the gallery. These could be a wall, but they are too close to the rocky ridge to be of any use. The entrance faces towards the northern slopes of Knocklayd Mountain, while to the north the western end of Rathlin Island can be seen on the horizon.

Mini-Gazetteer – 2.4km E there is a court tomb known as *Cloghafadd* at **Tervillen**. 7km S there is a stone pair at **Duncarbit**. 12.2km ESE there is a stone pair at **Ballycleagh**. 13.4km W there is a passage tomb at **Clegnagh**.

Ballyvoy
Passage Tomb
Grid Ref: D158 418 (Sheet 5)

Directions: *Head east from Ballycastle along the A2 for 3.5km and turn left at the crossroads. Continue to the farm at the end of the lane and ask for permission and directions.*

The kerb of Ballyvoy passage tomb.

All that remains of this fantastically located passage tomb is a low, almost complete kerb and a few stones set inside it. The kerb is 15m in diameter, constructed from stones up to 1m in length that stand up to 40cm proud of the ground. The only breaks in the kerb are in the south-east and north-east sections.

What this monument lacks in structural splendour it makes up for with fantastic views. To the north the site looks out to sea and Rathlin Island. To the south-west it is Knocklayd that, once again, dominates the horizon.

When complete this cairn could have stood up to 5m high, which would have presented a very imposing feature in the landscape for miles to the west. It would have also almost overpowered the court tomb on the slopes below (see above), which poses the following question about the destruction of this monument: was the material from this cairn used to provide the cairn that covered the tomb below or did the two sites co-exist intact? Depending upon the timeline for the monuments the opposite could, of course, be true and this passage tomb was built above the other monument and purposely placed to dominate it.

Mini-Gazetteer – (see previous site)

Beardiville – Gigmagog's Grave
Wedge Tomb
Grid Ref: C 907 373 (Sheets 4 & 5)

Directions: *From Ballymoney head north along the B62 towards Portrush. 5km after passing through Ballybogy the B17 goes off to the left, then shortly afterwards it heads off right. 300m past this junction there is a high hedge on the right-hand side of the road with a field gate. The tomb can be seen from this gate tucked away on the north-west corner of the field.*

A lot more of this monument is present than first meets the eye. This is because it is in an overgrown corner of a field with high hedges on two sides and some gorse bushes starting to encroach up the rear of the cairn. A significant amount of the cairn remains to the top of the gallery orthostats.

The north-east–south-west aligned gallery is about 4.5m long and nearly 1.5m wide. Two capstones remain in place towards the rear of the gallery and double walling can be seen on each side. The cairn is twice as long and twice as wide as the tomb. A field wall runs across the back edge of the cairn, not far from the rear of the gallery. The monument used to have wide views to the west, but the construction of a main road just 10m from it meant the erection of a high hedge that now blocks these totally.

The informal name for this site – *Gigmagog's Grave* – is very interesting. The name is probably a perversion of a name that goes back to biblical times – Gog and Magog, which appear in The Bible, 'Son of Man, set thy face against Gog, the land of

Beardiville wedge tomb.

Magog, the chief prince of Meshech and Tubal.'[68] In the twelfth century Geoffrey of Monmouth wrote of a giant called Gogmagog: 'Amongst the rest was one detestable monster, named Goemagot, in stature twelve cubits, and of such prodigious strength that at one shake he pulled up an oak as if it had been a hazel wand.'[69]

In this account Gogmagog is clearly a giant and many megalithic tombs are referred to as *Giant's Graves*, but how this name found its way to north Antrim is a mystery.

In some books the townland of this site is recorded as being Revallagh.

Mini-Gazetteer – 2.8km ENE there is a standing stone at *Flower Hill*. 3.8km WNW there is a standing stone at *Ballycraig*. 13km ENE there is a passage tomb at *Lemnagh Beg*. 15km SSW there is a portal tomb at Crevolea (Co. Derry).

Breen
Standing Stone
Grid Ref: D 122 340 (Sheet 5)

Directions: *From Armoy take the B15 east around the south of Knocklayd Mountain. After 5km enter the Breen Nature Reserve on the right-hand side of the road. Park near to the large barn. The stone can be seen from the track to the east of here.*

This is one of the many standing stones that seem to encircle Knocklayd Mountain. It is 1.6m tall, but a small pile of stone packed tightly around its base leaves only the top 1m of the stone visible. It is shaped like a cheese wedge standing on its broad end: the triangular sides facing north and south.

Standing next to the stone the presence of Knocklayd Mountain is not obviously, because the tall trees of a nearby plantation block the view to the north. However, moving just 100m away to the road that passes the field allows you to see the top of the seemingly ever-present mountain.

Mini-Gazetteer – 1.4km ENE there is a standing stone at *Corvally*. 5.1km NW there is a standing stone at *Ballylig*. 8.8km E there is a court tomb at *Ballyvennaght*. 10.3km NNE there is a standing stone at *Cross*.

Browndod 1
Court Tomb
Grid Ref: J 206 924 (Sheet 14)

Directions: *From Kells take the B98 east and then the B59 south. Turn right at the third crossroads. The tomb is on the top of the hill to the left and accessed via the third farm track on the left.*

Breen standing stone.

The gallery of Browndod 1 court tomb.

This impressively large court tomb has an electricity pylon towering over it that does not do the ambience of the site any favours. Once you have acclimatised yourself to its presence, however, the monument's finer points can be appreciated.

The west-facing court is in good condition with four large boulders forming the north side and three forming the south. A large, slightly displaced stone next to the north arm of the court is one of the entrance jambs. Next to the outer stone of the south arm of the 6m deep court there are two large stones forming the *façade*.

The gallery is an impressive 14m in length and is divided into four chambers by opposing jambs. The last two divisions have low sill stones between the jambs.

The trapezoidal cairn is 30m in length, extending 10m beyond the rear of the gallery to the base of the pylon. The remains of the cairn almost reach the tops of the gallery orthostats on the south side and although its outline on this side is quite distinct there is little visible evidence of a kerb.

Evans and Davies excavated the site in 1934. Three of the chambers were found to have been plundered, but the investigation of Chamber One did reveal evidence of paving. Chamber Three was undisturbed and the floor contained 'fragments of hazel or alder charcoal'. The level above the floor of this chamber contained fragments of pottery.[70]

The court area had been filled in with cairn material, perhaps in a decommissioning ceremony. The courts of the tombs at **Ballymacaldrack** and **Ballutoag** were similarly treated (see above).

Mini-Gazetteer – 1.2km WNW there is a standing stone in the same TD. 7.3km S there is a cairn at **Kilmakee**. 11.4km NW there is a court tomb at **Ballymarlagh**. 14.7km E there is a standing stone at **Ballygowan**.

Browndod 2
Court Tomb
Grid Ref: (Sheet 14)

Directions: *From Kells take the B98 east and then the B59 south. Turn right at the second crossroads. Continue to the next crossroads and turn left. After 1km the tomb can be seen on the hillside to the left, two fields back from the road.*

This, the lesser known of the Browndod court tombs, is not in as good a condition as the other. The gallery is all but destroyed and one side of the court is incomplete. The other side of the court comprises of seven large, impressive stones with little or no gaps between them. Adjacent to this arm of the court there are two more large stones from the *façade*. Where the entrance to the gallery would have been are two massive recumbent blocks of stone that were presumably the original entrance jambs.

Behind the court are the scant remains of the gallery, which is covered in what is left of the cairn. The few stones that are visible do not match the stones of the court

Browndod 2 court tomb.

in scale. The cairn can be traced back for approximately 10m from the back of the court, which again seems small in contrast to the large court stones.

The monument is built on a narrow shelf halfway up a south-facing slope and faces north-west into the hillside. The views to the south and south-east are very good.

Mini-Gazetteer – (see previous site)

Browndod – The Tardree Stone
Standing Stone
Grid Ref: J 196 930 (Sheet 14)

Directions: *This stone is difficult to reach and requires local knowledge. Ask in the area for directions.*

This stone is incorporated into a field boundary at the western extremity of the large number of monuments in this townland. It is 2m tall and has a shoulder-like protuberance on one side. When viewed from the west there is an anthropomorphic element to its appearance.

The hilltop position of the stone offers wonderful views, especially to the north where they are unbroken by hedgerows. In this direction Big Collin is the major landscape feature.

The Tardree Stone, Browndod.

Mini-Gazetteer – 1.2km ESE and 900m SE there are two court tombs in the same TD. 5.1km ESE there is a holed standing stone at **Holestone**. 10.2km ENE there is a court tomb at **Ballyalbaanagh**.

Cargan
Standing Stone
Grid Ref: D 168 172 (Sheet 9)

Directions: *From Ballymena take the A43 to the village of Cargan. At the crossroads in the village turn right and continue for 800m. The stone is on the left-hand side of the road between a house and its garage.*

This large, irregular stone stands just under 2m tall. It has been sandwiched in between a modern house and detached garage, taking in the role of a huge garden feature.

Mini-Gazetteer – 3.7km WSW there is a stone pair at **Lisnamanny**. 4km WSW there is a standing stone at **Skerry West**. 12.2km NNE there is a court tomb known as Ossian's Grave at **Lubitavish**. 12.5km WSW there is a standing stone at **Dromore**.

Cargan standing stone.

Carnanmore
Court Tomb
Grid Ref: D 034 380 (Sheet 5)

Directions: *From Ballymoney head north-east on the B147 through Stranocum. Continue along the B147 for 8km passing the junction with the B67. The tomb is on the left-hand side of the road just under 2km after the B67. If you reach a crossroads you have gone 200m too far.*

Note: *This is not the passage tomb popularly known as Carnanmore, but a court tomb in a different townland called Carnanmore. For the passage tomb see* **East Torr**.

From the roadside to the east this does not look like a very interesting site at all. From there it looks like a bush-covered mound with a fence around it. When viewed from the west, however, it changes completely. The south and west side of the remains are formed by huge boulders that form two walls of this ruined site. These stones are up to 2m in length and some are over 1.5m high.

The remains are so poor that its true classification is uncertain, but a court tomb seems the most likely.

Mini-Gazetteer – 5.7km E there is a standing stone at **Ballylig**. 6.1km N there is a cairn at **White Park**. 8.3km E there is a cairn on top of Knocklayd Mountain at **Tavnaghboy**. 12.7km W there is a wedge tomb known as *Gigmagog's Grave* at **Beardieville**.

The remains of Carnanmore court tomb.

Carncome
Standing Stone
Grid Ref: J 169 962 (Sheets 9 & 14)

Directions: *From Kells head east along the B98. The stone is on the side of the road 2km outside Kells.*

A 1.6m tall conglomerate standing stone that stands by the roadside. Sadly, any ambience that may have existed was torn away when the stone was incorporated into a modern redbrick wall. Instead of diverting the wall around the back of the stone and giving it some space someone decided to butt the wall right up to the stone on both sides.

Mini-Gazetteer – 5.1km SE there is a court tomb at ***Browndod***. 6.3km NNW there is a court tomb at ***Ballymarlagh***. 12km SSE there is a cairn at ***Kilmakee***. 13.3km N there is a court tomb at ***Loughconnelly***.

Clegnagh
Passage Tomb
Grid Ref: D 025 437 (Sheet 5)

Directions: *From Ballycastle follow the A2 northwards until it reaches the coast and turns sharply left. 1km after this turn there is a parking area on the right-hand side of the road.*

Carncome standing stone.

The tomb can be seen from here perched above a barn to the south-east. Access to the tomb is via the farmhouse next to the barns.

Of the three definite passage tombs along this stretch of coast, Clegnagh is the only one that is visible from the road, standing proud on a rocky knoll high above the nearby farmyard. The major factor in its visibility is the fact that the hillside in front of the tomb has been quarried away right up to the chamber, leaving it perched on the edge of a cliff. However, in its original form, with a cairn piled high over it the site would have easily been visible from below without any help from the quarry.

The eastern side of the monument is covered by thick gorse bushes, which hide any remains on that side. A modern fence runs across the rear of the area that would have originally been covered by the cairn. One large stone from the kerb is visible to the south-west of the chamber, measuring 1.5m long and 1m tall.

The chamber is represented by three 1m tall orthostats forming an open-sided box. Two of these are still upright while the third has collapsed under the capstone causing the latter to slip slightly. The open side of the chamber faces the edge of the quarry, making seeing into it quite difficult and rather precarious.

A quote in William Borlase's *The Dolmens of Ireland* refers to this ruined monument as, 'A small but very perfect cromlech'[71] – a far cry from what is to be seen today. The drawing that accompanies the entry does not include the '18 stones arranged in an

Clegnagh passage tomb.

oval, 32ft by 23ft', mentioned by O'Laverty in his *Historical Account of the Diocese of Down and Connor*[72], written in 1878.

Early reports of this monument identified the townland as being *Gleghnagh*[73] but this was presumably just a transcription error.

Mini-Gazetteer – 500m SW there is a passage tomb at **Lemnagh Beg**. 8.8km SE there is a standing stone at **Toberbile**. 13.4km E there is a passage tomb at **Ballyvoy**. 14.1km SE there is a standing stone at **Corvally**.

Cloghs – Cloghancor
Passage Tomb
Grid Ref: D 209 280 (Sheet 5)

Directions: *From Cushendall take the A2 north towards Ballycastle. Just 750m outside the town turn left and then immediately right at the first crossroads. Follow this lane for 2km and turn right and drive to the farm at the end of this track. Ask here for directions.*

Along with **Ballygawn** this is probably the least known of the east-coast monuments, despite being only 650m from *Ossian's Grave* at **Lubitavish** (as the crow flies), which is well frequented.

The design of this monument is akin to the small 'passageless' passage tombs along the north coast (see **Clegnagh**, **Lemnagh Beg** and **Magheraboy**). The chamber is small

Looking east over Cloghs passage tomb.

and defined by just five low orthostats. The single roofstone lies where it landed when it was thrown to one side when the tomb was opened. A south-facing gap in the orthostats defines the entrance. A circular raised area 8m or so in diameter can be traced around the tomb, which represents the extent of the cairn that once covered the structure, and some stones at the edge of this could represent the remains of a kerb.

Apart from its charm this site offers amazing views to the north over the glen, east towards the coast and south towards Tievebulliagh, the site of the famous porcellanite axe factory. To the north-east is Cross Slieve hill and just below this is the small, yet remarkable hill known as Tieverah.

Mini-Gazetteer – 650m NE there is a court tomb at *Lubitavish*. 6.7km NE there is a stone pair in *Ballycleagh*. 9.3km NNW there is a court tomb at *Glenmakeerin*. 12.6km N there is a passage tomb at *West Torr*.

Collinward
Cairn
Grid Ref: (Sheet   )

Directions: *The best route to this site is through the Cave Hill Country Park, but it is 1.5km off the newly laid walking route. Walk to McArt's Fort and then over the top of the nearest peak and across the valley to the transmitter masts.*

The levelled cairn at Collinward.

This cairn is only really for the completist to visit, as it has been severely damaged and robbed away. However, its hilltop position does offer fine views and the stretch of the Ulster Way through the valley below is a pleasure to walk along.

A tall transmitter mast towers over the site and the road to the mast has cut across one edge. The two standing stones on the cairn appear to be modern erections.

Mini-Gazetteer – 8.7km NNE there is a stone row known as *The Three Brothers* at *West Division*. 9.1 km WS there is a stone pair at ***Tornagrough***. 11.3km WNW there is a cairn at ***Kilmakee***. 14.2km ESE there is a portal tomb known as *The Kempe Stones* at Greengraves (Co. Down).

Corvally
Standing Stone
Grid Ref: D 134 348 (Sheet 5)

Directions: *From Armoy head east along the B15 skirting the south of Knocklayd Mountain. After 8km the road turns to the north. The stone is in a field to the left at this bend. Parking is very difficult here. Consult the OS map.*

This standing stone is just under 2m tall, but as it was re-erected in a bed of concrete in the 1950s it is no longer possible to say exactly how tall it originally stood. It stands

Corvally standing stone in its concrete setting with Knocklayd in the background.

on a barely perceptible mound, which was determined to be Neolithic in date during excavations carried out prior to the stone's re-erection.[74] It was found that the stone was placed on the mound at a later, but undeterminable date.

Flint chippings and a flint scraper were found nearby during pre-excavation field walks.

The location is on the foot-slopes of Knocklayd Mountain and is absolutely dominated by the hill's domed profile.

Mini-Gazetteer – 1.4km WSW there is a standing stone at **Breen**. 7.1km ENE there is a standing stone at **Ballyvennaght**. 9.3km ENE there is a passage tomb at **East Torr**. 13.2km NW there is a passage tomb known as *The Druid Stone* at **Magheraboy**.

Craigarogan – Carn Greine
Passage Tomb
Grid Ref: J 271 841 (Sheet 15)

Directions: *From the M2/A8(M) junction (Junction 4) to the west of Newtownabbey head west along the A6 towards Templepatrick for 3km and turn left. Continue for 1km passing a road to the left and take the next right. 300m along this road the tomb can be seen through a gate in a field to the right.*

Craigargan passage tomb.

Stylistically this is a unique monument in Northern Ireland as there are no others that are constructed in the same manner. It is closer in style to the Tramore group of passage tombs in Waterford or even the *Hunebedden* of The Netherlands.[75] The 10m long gallery is aligned north-east–south-west and is covered by six roofstones. At the south-west end of the monument there is a separate chamber (perhaps a later addition) that is separated from the rest of the gallery by a transverse slab. The top of the capstone on this chamber is 2m high.

Early descriptions of this monument state that it once had two stone circles surrounding it, 11 and 20m in diameter, that were destroyed in the eighteenth century. Another account mentions a ditch.[76] In 1914 H.C. Lawlor investigated the tomb and found evidence of cremation burials along the length of the gallery and an encrusted burial urn at its north-west end, which is now kept at Belfast Museum, 'In Carn Grania, directly under each of the top stones, were found the burned remains of one person, buried without urns; but close by, not under the covering stones, a large urn … was discovered, containing the incinerated remains of a woman.'[77]

Place names with Grania or Greine elements, such as Athgreany stone circle in Co. Wicklow, refer to the sun, so this monument is actually *The Cairn of the Sun*. Such references are usually attributed to sun worship or a long forgotten significant solar alignment at the site. As the structure is aligned north-east–south-west a summer solstice sunrise or winter solstice sunset alignment is possible here.

Visiting this monument can be quite disappointing. It stands in a field near to a hedgerow and is poorly tended. It will not be long before the brambles that are climbing over it consume it completely. This unique site should be made into a national monument, signposted and cared for properly for everyone to enjoy, perhaps following proper excavations.

Mini-Gazetteer – 6.2km SE there is a cairn at **Collinward**. 9km NW there is a stone circle at **Tobergill**. 10.7 km NW there is a court tomb at **Browndod**. 14.4km NNE there is a court tomb known as *Carndoo* at **Ballyboley**.

Craigs – The Broad Stone
Court Tomb
Grid Ref: C 979 176 (Sheet 8)

Directions: *The farm track that leads to this site is difficult to find. Ask locally for directions.*

This striking monument is well known from photographs, but is visited less frequently than others in the area because of a lack of signposts. Its roadside neighbour in **Craigs Lower** is easier to find and most people go no further. This is a National Monument with full access via a farm track and a short walk across a field.

The site is unusual for a court tomb, being located in a small, north–south aligned dip, which blocks the views in most directions. This must have been a conscious decision by the builders. The axis of the cairn is aligned north–south along this dip.

The Broad Stone, Craigs.

Two very impressive stones that are set at right angles to the monuments axis define the entrance to the small gallery. A narrow gap between these stones allows entry inside. The remains of the cairn are over 1m above the surrounding ground surface and the entrance jambs rise 1.3m above the top of this material – these are very large examples of entrance jambs. The currently visible extent of the cairn remains does not seem sufficient enough a base to have supported the amount of material needed to cover such a tall structure.

To one side of the entrance a single upright orthostat from the court is visible. Several metres in front of the entrance is a line of stones forming the *façade* of the cairn. Sections of the kerb can also be seen along both the north and south edges of the cairn.

One of the structural elements that give this monument such a striking profile is the large stone that forms the roof of the gallery today and gives the site its moniker: *The Broad Stone*. This was originally supported by five orthostats and was removed sometime prior to 1833[78] and replaced sometime in the late nineteenth century.

Mini-Gazetteer – 600m WSW there is a passage tomb at **Craigs Lower**. 4.3km E there is a court tomb known as *Dooey's Cairn* at **Ballymacaldrack**. 7.9km ESE there is a standing stone at **Dromore**. 13.8km E there is a standing stone at **Scotchomerbane**.

Craigs
Standing Stones
Grid Ref: C 977 183 (Sheet 8)

Directions: *These stones are difficult to find and require an OS map and GPS.*

There were once three standing stones clustered together here, but now only two remain. They measure 1.7m and 2.3m tall and both are incorporated into field boundaries.

In 1895 Wood-Martin mentioned these stones in his description of the *Broadstone*, a court tomb 800m to the south in the same townland, 'The Broadstone marks the grave of a giant; a little to the northward three large stones are said to mark the graves of three of his followers.'[79] Due to the tall hedgerows around these fields the stones are very difficult to see without jumping up and down a bit.

Mini-Gazetteer – 1km SSW there is a passage tomb at **Craigs Lower**. 8.1km NNE there is a standing stone at **Lisboy**. 8.5km SSE there is a standing stone at **Dromore**. 14km E there is a standing stone at **Scotchomerbane**.

The tallest of the three standing stones at Craigs.

Craigs Lower
Passage Tomb
Grid Ref: C 974 173 (Sheet 8)

Directions: *From Rasharkin take the B62 north. 800m after passing the junction with the B70 take a right turn. Follow this road to a t-junction and turn left. After 700m you come to a lane on the right-hand side of the road. The tomb is just inside the field through the gate opposite this lane and visible from the road.*

This monument looks like a large scuttling bug, frozen in time as it crosses the hillside. The large, thin capstone is held aloft by thin, leg-like orthostats, one of which has fallen.

At the entrance to the chamber there is a small stone, which represents the remains of a short passage. The capstone was repaired and re-erected during excavation in the mid-1980s after heavy frosts shattered it in the late 1970s.

The views from the site are all directed westwards, as the tomb stands at the top of a gentle west-facing slope.

Mini-Gazetteer – 1km NE there are three standing stones at **Craigs**. 8.5km W there is a passage tomb at Moneydig (Co. Derry). 9.1km NNE there is a standing stone at **Lisboy**. 15.4km WSW there is a court tomb at Cornaclery (Co. Derry).

Craigs Lower passage tomb.

Craigywarren standing stone.

Craigywarren
Standing Stone
Grid Ref: D 123 080 (Sheet 9)

Directions: *From Ballymena take the A43 north. 800m after passing beneath the motorway two roads go off to the left. Take the second of these. After 2km you will see the stone in a field on the right-hand side of the road.*

Slemish Mountain lies to the east of this short, squat stone and dominates the location. The stone is 1.2m tall and 1m thick. It is one of those stones that look different from every angle. It now stands in the centre of a field and serves as a rubbing post for cattle.

Mini-Gazetteer – 6.5km SSE there is a court tomb at **Ballymarlagh**. 7.6km N there is a stone pair at **Lisnamanny**. 11.5km ENE there is a portal tomb at **Ticloy**. 12.5km E there is a wedge tomb at **Tamybuck**.

Crockanore
Standing Stone
Grid Ref: D 189 418 (Sheet 5)

Directions: *This site requires an OS Map to locate.*

This 1m tall standing stone could be much more. The lumps and bumps along the small ridge that it stands on could be part of a plundered megalithic tomb. The stone does have the characteristics of a court tomb entrance jamb.

The location is an interesting one. The ground around the base of the rocky ridge is very waterlogged and it is possible that at one time the outcrop was surrounded by water, if not permanently then at least seasonally.

Mini-Gazetteer – 2.1km NW there is a standing stone at **Cross**. 3.1km W there is a court tomb at **Ballyvoy**. 8.9km SW there is a standing stone at **Corvally**. 13.9km S there is a passage tomb at **Cloghs**.

Cross
Passage Tomb
Grid Ref: D 171 431 (Sheet 5)

Directions: *This site requires a GPS, an OS map, local directions and a bit of luck to find. Access is via the farm 500m to the south of the site.*

Crockanore standing stone.

Looking down into Cross passage tomb.

This extremely small passage tomb was once 'the favourite retreat of badgers' and it was their presence that led to it being opened by 'sportsmen'.[80] When viewing the remains today it is easy to appreciate why – why the badgers liked it, that is, not why anyone would try to catch badgers in the name of 'sport'! The passage is very narrow and low and leads to a small oval chamber: the perfect place for a badger to chill out in.

The site is difficult to find on the rocky hilltop, because the orthostats are only 50cm high and the remains of the cairn reach nearly to their tops. There is a single roofstone lying in the passage and another lies to one side of the chamber. Some rocks forming an arc to the east may be all that's left of the site's kerb. The passage is aligned north–south with the entrance opening to the north. The eastern entrance stone is set at right angles to the passage, whereas its opposite number is in line with the passage orthostats.

The location is at the top of steep cliffs that plunge down to the sea below. This gives a great view over Rathlin Island to the north, and to Knocklayd and along the coast to the west.

Mini-Gazetteer – 900m ESE there is a crannog at *Lough-na-Crannagh*. 6.2km SSE there is a cairn at **Kilmakee**. 9.5km WSW there is a standing stone at **Ballylig**. 11.4km SW there is a standing stone at **Monanclogh**.

Cross
Standing Stone
Grid Ref: D 172 430 (Sheet 5)

Directions: *This site requires a GPS, an OS map, local directions and a bit of luck to find. Access is via the farm 500m to the south of the site.*

This standing stone is not marked on the OS maps and stands 150m away from the passage tomb in the same townland. It is the only erect stone amongst a field of prostrate boulders and stands 1.5m tall.

Mini-Gazetteer – (see previous site)

Dromore
Standing Stone
Grid Ref: D 048 137 (Sheet 8)

Directions: *From Clogh Mills take the A26 south and then the B64 west. When you meet the B93 turn right and head north. 300m after passing the junction with the B64 look into the fields to the left. The stone is quite difficult to see through the thick hedgerows.*

Above: Cross standing stone.

Left: Dromore standing stone.

This short basalt stone is just over 1m tall. It stands on the top of a small hill and is visible from the nearby road. It is roughly triangular in plan and aligned approximately north-east–south-west.

Mini-Gazetteer – 5.3km NNW there is a court tomb at ***Ballymacaldrack***. 8.5km ENE there is a standing stone at ***Scotchomerbane***. 8.2km WNW there is a passage tomb at ***Craigs Lower***. 12.5km NNW there is a standing stone at ***Lisboy***.

Duncarbit stone pair with Knocklayd Mountain in the distance.

Duncarbit
Stone Pair
Grid Ref: D 147 348 (Sheet 5)

Directions: *From Armoy head east along the B15 skirting the south of Knocklayd Mountain. After 8km the road turns to the north. 1.5km after the bend turn right along a road that doubles back to the south. Follow this narrow road for 1.5km to its highest point and ask for directions to the stones at one of the houses.*

No monument in Antrim is so dominated by Knocklayd Mountain as this fine stone pair. Knocklayd is a prominent landmark feature at many north Antrim sites, but here it is all you can see. The stones are situated on a level area on the west side of the wonderfully named Oghtbristacree Mountain facing and aligned to Knocklayd.

Both stones are 2m tall, but are very different in shape. The western stone is slender and tapers to a point, while the eastern stone is quite even in section. However, when viewed from the north the latter does broaden out and has the appearance of a spoon with its handle thrust into the ground.

The stones are aligned north-west–south-east and align towards the northern slopes of Knocklayd rather than pointing directly at its highest point as might be expected. This is a site where the possibility of an alignment to the Summer Solstice sunset over the edge of Knocklayd needs assessing.

Mini-Gazetteer – 5.7km ENE there is a portal tomb at ***Ballyvennaght***. 6.6km WNW there is a standing stone at ***Toberbile***. 9.2km SE there is a passage tomb at ***Cloghs***. 10km E there is a standing stone at ***Ballycleagh***.

Dunteige
Court Tomb
Grid Ref: D 323 085 (Sheet 9)

Directions: *From Larne take the A8 west and then head north along the B148. After 4.5km the road turns sharp right and a small road carries on ahead. 4km along this road you pass the Ulster Way car park. Continue for another 1.5km until you see a new field gate on the right-hand side of the road next to a left-hand bend. The tomb is visible up the hill from this gate.*

Very little of this difficult-to-reach monument survives. Just four of the orthostats are still standing, whereas an early photograph shows that it once had a lintelled entrance leading into a single chamber.[81] The remains of the 17m cairn can be traced behind the structure.

The monument, then called *Cairnasegart*, was investigated in 1870 by Dr J. S. Holden and Lord Antrim, when two lozenge shaped arrowheads, seventeen flint implements and four Neolithic urns containing cremations were found. At this time the monument was described as being 'constructed of eight standing stones, close together, forming a

Dunteige court tomb.

small lozenge-shaped enclosure with a large slab lying partially on top like a cromlech.'[82]

The site is on a west-facing slope high on the side of a north–south aligned valley through which Linford Water runs. 250m to the north of the court tomb is Craigy Hill, a large rocky prominence that almost overpowers the site.

Mini-Gazetteer – 2.2km NNE there is a standing stone at **Ballygilbert**. 4.4km SSE there is a standing stone at **Killyglen**. 7.2km WNW there is a court tomb at **Antynanum**. 12.7km ESE there is a passage tomb at **Ballylumford**.

Dunteige
Wedge Tomb
Grid Ref: D 323 080 (Sheet 9)

Directions: *From Larne take the A8 west and then head north along the B148. After 4.5km the road turns sharp right and a small road carries on ahead. 4km along this road you pass the Ulster Way car park. Continue for another 1.5km until you see a new field gate on the right-hand side of the road next to a left-hand bend. The tomb is visible up the hill from this gate.*

Situated on a small rise to the south of a tall rock eminence known as Craigy Hill, this site has great views to the south. The entrance to the 5m long gallery is aligned west-south-west, roughly in the direction of Slemish Mountain. The front of the tomb

Dunteige wedge tomb.

has some stones from its *façade* in place, behind which there is a split portico and antechamber that has a single upright dividing its entrance. Behind the portico, a slab, leaving the other side open, blocks one side of the main gallery's entrance.

The gallery has double walling on the eastern side and a jamb stone projects half-way across the gallery from this wall. The rear of the gallery is ruined and there is no sign of any kerbstones.

Not far away there is a Mass rock: a stone used as an altar during penal times. This has a lovely cross inscribed on its north face. The stone does not appear to have been taken from the wedge tomb, but the choice of position for these then illegal Masses is interesting. Presumably, the tomb was a handy landmark when giving directions to the site.

Mini-Gazetteer – (see previous site)

East Torr – Carnanmore or Carnlea
Passage Tomb
Grid Ref: D 218 388 (Sheet 5)

Directions: *This monument is best approached from the north, although other routes are available. This route is the most gentle, but can be boggy in places and involves crossing two barbed-wire-topped fences, one of which has a stile. Park at the road junction at D 211 404 and walk south along the gentle slopes of the mountain. This route is a little over 1.5km long.*

Unlike its neighbour at **West Torr** this passage tomb is in fairly good condition. The cairn still covers the passage and most of the chamber. Regretfully, entry into the tomb was not sought via the passage, but by removing the front portion of the chamber's roof. There is, however, a small silver lining: the opening does allow a rare view of a corbelled roof in section, something that can otherwise only be seen in the passage tomb on Seefin, Co. Wicklow.

The tops of the passage orthostats can be seen as they pass through the cairn to the chamber, but the passage itself is filled with cairn material. A few roofstones from the passage are also slightly exposed and a group of large stones in front of the passage represent the missing roofstones from the passage and chamber. The alignment of the passage is westwards and points at the northern edge of Knocklayd Mountain's domed summit.

The chamber floor is 1.5m x 1.5m and there is about 2m headroom below the large central roofstone. Below this stone, large slabs form the corbelled roof in a much cruder fashion than the corbelled roof at Newgrange, Co. Meath.

There are two decorated stones at **East Torr**. One of these is the slab immediately behind and underneath the topmost stone. The decoration on this slab is oddly on the outside and consists of spirals and a zig-zag motif. These cannot be seen today, because

East Torr passage tomb as seen when you approach from the east.

they are very worn and now covered over by cairn material. The other decorated stone is to the south of the topmost roofstone and again immediately below it. The upper surface of this slab is dotted with cup-marks and these continue around one side and on to the underside. This shows that the stone was decorated before being placed in its current location within the structure.

From the top of this mountain the views are as good as they get. To the west stands Knocklayd and out to sea you overlook Rathlin Island and to the extreme north the Scottish island of Islay. The Scottish mainland is visible to the north-east.

Thankfully, the concrete Ordnance Survey trig point that was placed on the top of the cairn has fallen over and so does not spoil the profile of this spectacular monument.

Mini-Gazetteer – 1.9km NNW there is a passage tomb at *West Torr*. 3.8km WSW there is a court tomb at *Glenmakeerin*. 6.7km WNW there is a court tomb at *Ballyvoy*. 10.6km WSW there is a cairn on top of Knocklayd Mountain at *Tavnaghboy*.

Flower Hill
Standing Stone
Grid Ref: C 934 382 (Sheets 4 & 5)

Directions: *From Bushmills head south-west on the B17 towards Coleraine and turn left at the first crossroads. After a little over 1km you pass a farm track on the left and reach another*

Flower Hill standing stone.

farm track on the right. Drive up this to the farmyard and ask to visit the stone, which is in the field across the track from the farmhouse.

The size of this stone is impressive. By volume it is possibly the largest stone in Co. Antrim: standing 2.5m tall, over 2m wide and more than 1m thick. The top of the stone is very uneven, having two peaks, perhaps indicating that it was broken in antiquity. How big was this stone when it was first erected?

It stands on a ridge that runs north–south and would have had fine views all around. The many farm buildings that crowd around it now interrupt these, but the view to the east remains fairly open, allowing a clear view to Knocklayd Mountain.

The stone is aligned close to north–south along the axis of the ridge.

Mini-Gazetteer – 6km W there is a standing stone at ***Ballycraig***. 10km E there is a court tomb at ***Carnanmore***. 10.6km ENE there is a passage tomb at ***Clegnagh***. 14.8km SSE there is a standing stone at ***Lisboy***.

The north gallery of Glenmakeerin court tomb.

Glenmakeerin
Court Tomb
Grid Ref: D 184 370 (Sheet 5)

Directions: *This site needs an OS map to find, despite being signposted within Ballypatrick Forest Park to the north-west of Cushendun. Directions once in the park are very difficult.*

This monument is buried deep inside Ballypatrick Forest and as it is Antrim's only double court tomb, you would think that it would be better cared for. The only allowance that has been made is not planting trees on top of it, but there are trees right up to its edges – hopefully when this part of the plantation is cleared a lot more room will be left clear from future planting.

Both galleries are in poor condition, neither being complete. Some of the cairn remains, but this is overgrown with heather and reeds making it very difficult to see the site properly. The close-set trees add to the difficulty of appreciating what is actually in front of you: room to stand back and look at the site as a whole would make this site much better.

Mini-Gazetteer – 1.6km E there is a double portal tomb at **Ballyvennaght**. 3.8km ENE there is a passage tomb at **East Torr**. 7.3km ESE there is a stone pair at **Ballycleagh**. 15km W there is a court tomb at **Carnanmore**.

Goakstown or Ault
Standing Stone
Grid Ref: D 315 107 (Sheet 9)

Directions: *Despite being very close to Glenarm, directions to this site are a bit tricky – please look at the OS map to follow them. From Glenarm head up the hill to the south. Take the right-hand turn a little under 1km south of Glenarm and follow the road for 4.5km where you will come to a GAA pitch on the right. The stone is in the next field to the south.*

On the hillside above this stone is the much more interesting wedge tomb in the same townland. If you are visiting the tomb then take time to look at this stone, but do not go out of your way to visit it. The stone's location makes it very unappealing, as it is in the centre of a field, surrounded by neat hedges. It is fairly nondescript and stands around 1.5m tall.

The stone does have one redeeming feature, though: the view to the south-west is dominated by Slemish Mountain and the stone is on a direct line between the wedge tomb and Slemish.

Goakstown standing stone with Slemish in the background.

Mini-Gazetteer – 2.3km SSE there is a court tomb at ***Dunteige***. 3.2km ESE there is a passage tomb at ***Ballygawn***. 6.8km W there is a wedge tomb at ***Tamybuck***. 13.5km S there is a court tomb known as *Carndoo* at ***Ballyboley***.

Goakstown or Ault
Wedge Tomb
Grid Ref: D 316 108 (Sheet 9)

Directions: *Despite being very close to Glenarm, directions to this site are a bit tricky – please look at the OS map to follow them. From Glenarm head up the hill to the south. Take the right hand turn a little under 1km south of Glenarm and follow the road for 4.5km where you will come to a GAA pitch on the right. The tomb is near to the farm building along the next track on the left.*

Goakstown wedge tomb is one of the monuments that should be a National Monument with full public access. It is a large monument that is in good condition and has many interesting features. As it is, the monument is not really looked after and large gorse bushes have been allowed to grow on top of it.

The gallery is 10m long and has fine double walling. The outer orthostats are massive and stand 5m wide at the southern end, tapering to 4m wide at the rear. In front of the gallery there is a portico, to one side of which stands a large *façade* stone. The inner walls that form the internal gallery are only 1m apart, making it very narrow. In 2003 it was possible to see some of the internal structure from above, but the gorse bushes now hide most of this. There is one roofstone still *in situ* towards the rear of the gallery.

The monument's most interesting feature is the slab that separates the portico from the main gallery. A large piece of the top left-hand corner of this slab is missing. The gap is sufficient to have allowed entry into the main gallery, perhaps for inserting and removing remains on special occasions.

Goakstown wedge tomb.

The field hedge that stands just a few metres in front of the tomb doesn't really block any views, but it does prevent you seeing the monument properly from the farm track on the opposite side. The views here are all about the south-west. The slope that the monument stands on is west facing, forcing the observer to look in that direction where Slemish Mountain stands large and proud.

Mini-Gazetteer – 3.7km SSE there is a cairn at **Ballycoos**. 5.5km W there is a stone pair known as *The Maidens* at **Antynanum**. 8.4km W there is a portal tomb at **Ticloy**. 14.7km SE there is a passage tomb at **Ballylumford**.

Holestone – Doagh or The Hole Stone
Standing Stone
Grid Ref: J 242 907 (Sheet 14)

Directions: *From Antrim take the B95 west and pass beneath the motorway until you reach Parkgate. 150m after passing the church in Parkgate turn left and follow the road around until you reach the B59. Turn left and head north for just over 1km and turn right. The stone is signposted on the right-hand side of the road after 500m.*

This famous stone has been left to its own devices in recent years and is now surrounded by thick gorse bushes. At one time, when you entered the field, the stone stood proud and silhouetted in front of you, but now you have to climb onto the rocky outcrop on which it stands to see it.

The stone is 1.5m tall and has a 10cm wide dumb-bell-shaped hole pierced through it around 1m from its base. At one time the site was used for making pledges, especially those of marriage. The two parties would join hands through the hole and make their oath. In 1830 McSkimin wrote, 'It is still deemed a place consecrated to the meeting of lovers, and when they join their hands through the stone, the pledge of love and troths there given is sacred.'[83]

It is easy to picture the happy couple and a few close friends standing on top of the 4m tall rocky outcrop, holding hands through the stone, while the rest of the congregation stand below watching the ceremony: at least it would be if the gorse were cleared allowing the stone to be seen once again from below.

The site is clearly ancient and the giving of oaths into Victorian times is probably an echo of ancient oath-giving practices. It is equally easy to picture two tribal chiefs meeting here and making a peace treaty while the armies stood below. The site could also have been one of the many inaugural sites for local kings.

Mini-Gazetteer – 4km WNW there is a court tomb at **Browndod**. 6km SSW there is a cairn at **Kilmakee**. 9.1km NW there is a standing stone at **Carncome**. 11.7km ENE there is a standing stone at **Ballygowan**.

The Hole Stone standing stone.

Killyglen
Standing Stone
Grid Ref: D 337 043 (Sheet 9)

Directions: *From Larne take the A2 towards Belfast and then the B148 north. After 1km the road turns sharply right. Continue along the B148 for 750m and turn left at the next crossroads. The stone is on the left-hand side of the road after 4.5km, near to where the Ulster Way footpath crosses it.*

At over 2m tall this is one of the largest standing stones in Co. Antrim. It stands on open ground to the north of Agnew's Hill, a large round-topped mountain. The stone itself occupies a spot close to the highest point in a mountain pass and could well have been placed here as a way-marker or a boundary stone.

Being close to the Ulster Way footpath makes it a well-known landmark, but this does have its downside; in 2004 paint was thrown over the stone in an act of mindless vandalism.[84]

Mini-Gazetteer: 4km WNW there is a wedge tomb at **Dunteige**. 6.5km N there is a court tomb at **Lisnahay South**. 6.8km NNW there is a wedge tomb at **Goakstown**. 10.9km SSE there is a standing stone at **Ballynarry**.

Killyglen standing stone.

Kilmakee
Cairn
Grid Ref: J 218 852 (Sheet 14)

Directions: *From Antrim follow the A6 east towards Templepatrick. 800m after passing through Dunadry you will come to a farm lane on the left. The easiest way to get to this site is to drive up to the farmhouse and ask for directions.*

At first sight it is difficult to appreciate this monument's splendour. This is because, at some time, someone thought it was a good idea to plant sycamore and beech trees around the circumference of this robbed-out cairn. The roots of these large trees spill out over the kerb almost obscuring them in places.

The cairn is over 30m in diameter and reduced in height to the level of the forty-five green basalt kerbstones. One of the kerbstones may have cupmarks carved on it, which could point to this monument being a passage tomb, but there is no sign of a central structure. Most of the kerb is present except for a few stones on the north-eastern edge. The kerbstones are massive, up to 2m in length and over 1.5m tall.

Mini-Gazetteer – 5.4km N there is a stone circle at **Tobergill**. 9.2km SE there is a court tomb known as *Hanging Thorn Cairn* at **Ballyutoag**. 12km NNW there is a standing stone at **Carncome**. 14.2km NNE there is a court tomb at **Ballyalbaanagh**.

Kilmakee cairn as you first see it across the field.

Lemnagh Beg/Lemnaghbeg – Cloghnaboghil
Passage Tomb
Grid Ref: D 022 433 (Sheet 5)

Directions: *From Bushmills head east along the A2 to White Park Bay. 500m past the car park and youth hostel you will pass a road to the right. Access to the tomb is via the farm 500m on the right past this road.*

This is the most westerly of the three passage tombs above White Park Bay. It is also, arguably, the most complete, although that at *Magheraboy* is more picturesque.

Much of this monument's 7m diameter kerb still exists. The central chamber is still mainly embedded into the base of the cairn, which remains to the height of the kerb. There are four orthostats forming a chamber about 1.5m x 80cm and 60cm deep. These four stones are arranged so that an opening has been left at the east end of the chamber. The capstone is still in place and measures 2m x 1.5m.

As with all the passage tombs around White Park Bay, the views are fantastic. To the west you can look along the coast past the bay below and on a clear day it is possible to see Scotland to the east. The site is near to the top of one of the highest points for some distance, but its placement on north-facing slopes means that the inland view is disrupted by slightly higher ground. The focus of attention at this site is all about the sea.

The chamber of Lemnagh Beg passage tomb.

In 1884 Gray wrote, 'This is the smallest cromlech in the north-east of Ireland. Its local name Cloghnabohil, signifies the stone of the boy … From the open and elevated position of this cromlech there is a very extended prospect seaward, including a considerable portion of the west coast and islands of Scotland.'[85] The drawing that accompanied Gray's description, like many early drawings of monuments, was not terribly accurate, showing more of the chamber orthostats above ground than is the case and the capstone being much too thick.

Mini-Gazetteer – 1.6km ENE there is a passage tomb known as *The Druid Stone* at *Magheraboy*. 8.8km SE there is a standing stone at *Toberbile*. 12.8km E there is a stone pair at *Ballynaglogh*. 13km WSW there is a wedge tomb known as *Gigmagog's Grave* at *Beardieville*.

Lisboy
Standing Stone
Grid Ref: D 011 256 (Sheets 5,8)

Directions: *From Ballymoney take the B16 east for 4.5km and turn right. Shortly afterwards you will go over a crossroads and the road will bend around to the right. The stone is in a field to the left just after this bend.*

Lisboy standing stone.

This small, rough stone stands at the centre of a modern field near to the base of a small hillock. High hedgerows and houses block the views in all directions, leaving this 1.5m tall stone without a sense of place or purpose.

Mini-Gazetteer – 7.4km S there is a court tomb known as *Dooey's Cairn* at *Ballymacaldrack*. 8.1km SSW there are three standing stones at *Craigs*. 9.1km SSW there is a passage tomb at *Craigs Lower*. 15km SE there is a standing stone at *Skerry West*.

Lisnahay South
Court Tomb
Grid Ref: D 341 108 (Sheet 9)

Directions: *From Ballygally follow the coast road north for 6km and turn south along the B148. Turn right into the third farm track (about 1.3km) and ask at the farm for directions.*

As you approach this monument it does not look very impressive, because only a few of the remaining stones stand more than 50cm proud of the surrounding land. A visit during the spring or summer would make it even more difficult to see anything, because the site is enshrouded in bracken during this time. During the winter, however, it is easy to see the great features that are present.

Looking into the court of Lisnahay South.

The monument is aligned north–south with a 5m wide and 6m deep V-shaped court at the north end. Some of the *façade* stones can be seen on both sides of the court, but they are better preserved on the west side. Two well-matched entrance jambs lead into the first and only remaining chamber of the gallery. This 2m long chamber is slightly oval in plan and has been dug out to a depth of 40cm, revealing a sillstone between the entrance jambs.

About 5m behind the remains of the gallery there are two subsidiary chambers set at right angles to the axis of the cairn. The east subsidiary chamber is formed by five orthostats and has no backstone. The west chamber is more complete, having a back stone and what looks like a doorstone in front of it, too.

Very little of the retaining kerb remains in place making it difficult to judge how long the cairn was originally. There are two possible lines of stones running across the cairn either of which could mark its back edge, but it is impossible to tell. The two lines could indicate that the cairn was extended at some time, perhaps when the two subsidiary chambers were built.

The tomb was built at the base of a steep slope, which totally obscures the views to the west. The field rises to the north and slightly to the east, limiting the view in those directions. To the south a small stretch of coastline around Ballygaley Head is visible.

Mini-Gazetteer – 800m WSW there is a standing stone at ***Ballygilbert***. 2.9km SW there is a court tomb at ***Dunteige***. 8.5km W there is a court tomb at ***Antynanum***. 13.6km S there is a passage tomb known as *Carndoo* at ***Ballyboley***.

Lisnamanny
Stone Pair
Grid Ref: D 135 155 (Sheet 9)

Directions: *From Ballymena take the A43 north for 10km and turn left at the crossroads. After 1km the road forks – keep left. 400m past the fork there is a bungalow on the right with a track alongside it. The stones are just up this track.*

These two stones are now separated by a relatively modern farm track that runs between them, making them look like ancient gateposts. Each is about 1.5m tall. Their alignment is roughly south-east to north-west across the line of the valley formed by the Clogh River.

The pair is part of a cluster of eight standing stone sites within a 4km radius, which are mainly located on the northern side of the valley. The site is overlooked by the cairn-topped Carncormick Mountain, which is roughly to the south-east, although the pair's axis does not align to its peak.

Mini-Gazetteer – 1km NW there is a standing stone at **Skerry West**. 3.7km ENE there is a standing stone at **Cargan**. 10.4km ESE there is a portal tomb at **Ticloy**. 14.5km NNE there is a passage tomb at **Cloghs**.

One of the stones from
Lasnamanny stone pair.

Loughconnelly - Neenrowes Knowe
Court Tomb
Grid Ref: D 190 093 (Sheet 9)

Directions: *From Broughshane follow the A42 east for 4km taking the third turning on the left. This road turns sharply right after 1.5km. A further 500m along the road there is a lane to the right with a signpost to Skerry Graveyard. 200m further on, the next lane on the right leads to the tomb. While you are in the area be sure to walk up to Skerry Graveyard and check out the views!*

Although reported in the 1940s, this tomb was thought to have been lost to field clearance. However, it is still here, but very difficult to make out. The covering cairn has been trimmed to a triangular shape and walled in with 1.5m tall dry-stone walls. Amongst all the other beautiful dry-stone walls in the area it is very difficult to make out from a distance.

A farm track runs right past the west side of the cairn and it is alongside this road that you can see the real evidence of the tomb's presence. Incorporated into the wall are two large, upright stones that were once the entrance into a subsidiary chamber. Traces of the chamber's internal structure can be seen behind these stones, but the chamber itself is filled in.

Just behind the wall on the south side of the site there are several large slabs that could be part of the main structure.

Mini-Gazetteer – 5.7km E there is a wedge tomb at **Tamybuck**. 8.3km NW there is a stone pair at **Lisnamanny**. 9km SSW there is a court tomb at **Ballymarlagh**. 14.9km WNW there is a standing stone at **Dromore**.

Lubitavish – Ossian's Grave or Cloghbrack
Court Tomb
Grid Ref: D 213 285 (Sheet 5)

Directions: *From Cushendall take the A2 north. After approximately 2km turn left and continue for 1km where you will reach a track on the left that crosses a flat bridge. Park here and walk through the farmyard and up the hill. This track winds up the hill. Near to the top you will find a kissing gate on the right and the tomb is in the field beyond this.*

This is a popular monument with tourists and features in many guides to the area. Reaching it is not easy, as it requires a tough walk up a steep, winding farm track. It is not very well signposted either.

As you enter the field the first impression is not a particularly overwhelming one: the remains are low and slightly downhill from you, making them seem very small.

These two stones are the only visible trace of Loughconnelly court tomb.

Ossian's Grave at Lubitavish.

Closer inspection is at first confusing, because the orthostats of the gallery are in some disarray. The site has no cairn remaining, giving the site a neglected, forgotten and skeletal look. There is no information sign.

The tomb's court is quite well represented with each arm of the court being almost complete. A fine pair of jamb stones marks the entrance into the gallery. This has two chambers separated by jamb stones that project inwards to leave a narrow opening. None of the stones are more than 1m tall above the current field level.

The court faces up the slope of the hill, which rises sufficiently to obscure the view to the south, which would otherwise include Tievebulliagh, the site of the axe factory. To the east you can see the *fairy hill* of Tieveragh above Cushendall.

From the tomb, a rock outcrop is visible, which could easily be the source of the stone used to build this monument.

Mini-Gazetteer – 6km NE there is a stone pair at **Ballycleagh**. 9.1km NW there is a stone pair at **Duncarbit**. 10.6km WNW there is a standing stone at **Breen**. 12.1km N there is a passage tomb at **West Torr**.

Magheraboy, The Druid Stone or Mount Druid
Passage Tomb
Grid Ref: D 037 438 (Sheet 5)

Directions: *From Bushmills head east along the A2 to White Park Bay. 2km past the car park and youth hostel the A2 turns sharply left and the B15 continues ahead. Take the B15 and then the first right-hand turn after 300m. The tomb is on the top of the hill behind a cottage 800m along this lane.*

Of the three north Antrim passage tombs that overlook White Park Bay, this is the best known. Its local name, *The Druid Stone*, conjures images of priestly folk sacrificing virgins with golden sickles under a full moon. The truth, of course, could not have been more different, but romantics will be romantics and early antiquarians were amongst the most romantic of them all.

This is an attractive tomb, which has been photographed and sketched many times. The capstone is raised high enough above the ground level to make it look imposing in a low-angle photograph. The monument's name and its aesthetic appeal have made it a favourite Antrim site for a long time.

The monument itself is in good order. The cairn has been removed to the level of the surrounding kerb, leaving the central chamber standing around 1.5m tall. The chamber itself measures about 1.5m x 1.5m in plan and 1m tall. The capstone rests on three orthostats, a fourth having fallen into the chamber. A short stone to the north of the chamber could be the remnants of a short passage. The orthostats supporting the 2m long capstone each has a flat surface facing inwards, creating a very neat chamber.

The Druid Stone at Magheraboy.

The kerb is 12m in diameter and completes an arc from south to north-west, while enough stones remain around the rest of the kerb's line to follow its course as far as the north-east. Here it meets a dry-stone wall that cuts off one edge of the cairn.

Excavations here by J.M. Mogey in June 1939 produced some interesting results. The remaining cairn material contained large amounts of flint flakes and a flint knife. Beneath the cairn there was a layer of blackened earth with charcoal. In front of the chamber there were some burnt bone and round quartz pebbles mixed in with the cairn material. The chamber itself had been 'thoroughly rifled'. Some of the packing stones around the orthostats showed signs of burning, leading the excavator to surmise that the blackened layer of charcoal bearing soil mentioned above was the result of burning that took place on site. The pottery finds included Neolithic and Bronze Age wares.[86]

No date is available for the construction of the site, but further investigation should be able to produce enough charcoal to give a date through radiocarbon dating techniques.

Mini-Gazetteer – 1.4km W there is a cairn at *White Park*. 7.9km SE there is a standing stone at *Ballylig*. 11.5km ESE there is a stone pair at *Ballynaglogh*. 13.2km SE there is a standing stone at *Corvally*.

Monanclogh standing stone.

Monanclogh
Standing Stone
Grid Ref: D 083 358 (Sheet 5)

Directions: *From Armoy head north on the A44 towards Ballycastle. Turn right after 2km and then immediately left. After 1km you pass a road to the right. The standing stone is in a field behind a farmhouse on the right 500m past this junction.*

At 1.5m tall this is one of the shortest standing stones around Knocklayd Mountain. It is of very uneven profile, looking different from every angle. It is situated at the base of a field just above a steep slope that marks the western edge of Knocklayd Mountain. Farm buildings up the slope to the east next to the road almost block the views of Knocklayd itself, but there are fine, expansive views to the west if you look through the hedgerow that runs across the slope just 2m from the stone.

Mini-Gazetteer – 3.3km E there is a cairn on top of Knocklayd Mountain at *Tavnaghboy*. 6.5km E there is a stone pair at **Duncarbit**. 9.6km NE there is a passage tomb at **Ballyvoy**. 11.6km ENE there is a court tomb known as *Cloghafadd* at *Tervillin*.

Scotchomerbane
Standing Stone
Grid Ref: D117 175 (Sheet 9)

Directions: *From Clogh Mills take the B94 south to Clogh and then turn left along the B64. After 3km you come to a crossroads. Turn left and continue until you come to a farmhouse on the left-hand side after 1.5km. The stone is a few metres past these buildings on the same side of the road.*

Being built into a roadside dry-stone wall this 2m tall stone is easy to visit. It is very rough and unshaped – what at one time would certainly have been described as a 'rude stone monument'.

There is a depression or notch running from the front to the back of the stone across its top, giving it a phallic (if rather warty) appearance.

Mini-Gazetteer – 5.1km E there is a standing stone at ***Cargan***. 9.6km W there is a court tomb known as *Dooey's Cairn* at ***Ballymacaldrack***. 13.8km W there is a court tomb known as *The Broadstone* at ***Craigs***. 14.9km ESE there is a stone pair at ***Antynanum***.

Scotchomerbane standing stone.

Skerry West
Standing Stone
Grid Ref: D 129 163 (Sheet 9)

Directions: *From Clogh Mills take the B94 south to Clogh and then turn left along the B64. After 3km you come to a crossroads and then a road to the right. The stone is in the field just past this second road.*

Like the nearby stone at **Scotchomerbane**, this 1.8m-tall standing stone has a grooved top, giving it a phallic appearance when viewed from the east. As you move around the stone it changes shape seemingly from every direction, because it has a very uneven profile. The west side has a step at around 1m high, similar to many found on the portal stones of some portal tombs.

There are many stones throughout this valley making it a very productive area to visit.

Mini-Gazetteer – 1.7km NW there is a standing stone at **Scotchomerbane**. 8.3km S there is a standing stone at **Craigywarren**. 11.2km ESE there is a portal tomb at **Ticloy**. 14.8 km NE there is a court tomb known as *Ossian's Grave* at **Lubitavish**.

Skerry West standing stone.

The gallery of Tamybuck wedge tomb.

Tamybuck
Wedge Tomb
Grid Ref: D 247 099 (Sheet 9)

Directions: *From Carnlough take the A42 south-east towards Broughshane. 2km after passing the junction with the B97, the A42 turns right at a crossroads: turn left here and continue for 2km until you reach a road on the right. The tomb is hidden from view by a dry-stone wall two fields back from between the two roads.*

This is a difficult site to decipher. The remains of the gallery are very clear and quite well preserved, but it is what is happening around the structure that is confusing. The gallery is about 5m long and 1m wide internally. The orthostats forming the walls are mostly long, rounded boulders, while the remaining displaced roofstone is rough and undressed. On the north side the double walling of the gallery is very obvious, while on the south side it is hardly evident at all. The cairn remains to the tops of the orthostats.

About 20m from the west end of the gallery the ground drops sharply by 4m. Between the end of the gallery and this drop there has been much quarrying, leaving a deep scar. Within the quarry dip there are many large stones that could have come from the tomb. There are what appear to be traces of the cairn beyond the quarry area, making it over 40m long.

In the field below the tomb there is a low, circular enclosure with a small standing stone set off centre.

Mini–Gazetteer – 1.4km NE there is a court tomb at *Antynanum*. 9.1km E there is a cairn at *Ballygawn*. 12.5km W there is a standing stone at *Craigywarren*. 13.1km SSE there is a court tomb at *Ballyalbaanagh*.

Tavnaghboy – Carn-na-Truagh
Cairn
Grid Ref: D 115 364 (Sheet 5)

Directions: *There are many ways to climb Knocklayd, but one of the easiest is from the car park in Ballycastle Forest on the eastern side (D 130 377). From the car park, walk along the tracks keeping left until you reach the far edge of the forest and the base of the hill. Walk along the edge of the forest until you reach a wall that climbs straight up the hill. From here walk up the hill keeping the wall to your left.*

This massive hilltop cairn probably houses a passage tomb similar to those at *West Torr* and *East Torr*. The cairn is 3m tall and 18m in diameter, and is topped off with an OS trig point. The south and south-west sides of the cairn have been eroded by the prevailing wind exposing a fabulous kerb made of massive blocks of stone laid flat against the sloping mound rather than set upright into the ground. The other sides of the cairn are now grass and peat covered, which hides the large quantity of quartz used in its construction.[87] When first constructed this site must have shone when the sunshine

Tavnaghboy cairn on Knocklayd Mountain.

fell upon it. The importance of this effect is further highlighted by the fact that the cairn is positioned so that it is most easily seen from the south of the mountain.

Knocklayd is a vast dome-like mountain that looks very breast-like. The cairn helps to emphasise this effect in much the same way that the cairns on Seefin (Co. Wicklow) and Seahan (Co. Dublin) do.

On a good day the views from here are extensive. To the west and south the plains of Antrim open up, while to the east lie the Glens of Antrim. Fair Head is prominent to the north-east and there is a wonderful view northwards to Rathlin Island, the chalk cliffs of which light up spectacularly in the sun.

Mini-Gazetteer – 2.5km SE there is a standing stone at **Corvally**. 6.8km NE there is a passage tomb at **Ballyvoy**. 8.7km NE there is a passage tomb at **Cross**. 10.7km ENE there is a passage tomb at **West Torr**.

Tervillin
Cairn
Grid Ref: D 179 423 (Sheet 5)

Directions: *From Ballycastle head east along the A2 towards Cushendun. At the crossroads in Ballyvoy continue straight on, leaving the main road. Turn left at the first opportunity and continue for 2.5km where you will see the cairn on the left-hand side of the road with Lough-na-Crannagh beyond.*

Although situated close to the picturesque shore of *Lough-na-Crannagh* and close to the foot of a waterfall, this site is a disappointment. It is a low, robbed out cairn with several stones protruding from it, which may have once been orthostats from a tomb.

Mini-Gazetteer – 1.1km NW there is a passage tomb at **Cross**. 2.2km WSW there is a court tomb at **Ballyvoy**. 6.4km SE there is a portal tomb at **Ballyvennaght**. 11.3km SE there is a stone pair at **Ballycleagh**.

Tervillin (Cloghafadd)
Court Tomb
Grid Ref: D 182 418 (Sheet 5)

Directions: *This site is high on the hill to the south of the previous site. Ask for directions at the farm nearby.*

In 1940 this court tomb was described as a 'mutilated horned cairn … almost hidden in rank heather on a rocky knoll'.[88] This does not provide a lot of inspiration for a

Tervillin cairn with Lough-na-Crannagh beyond.

Tervillin court tomb.

visit, but luckily its situation has changed since then. The field that the tomb is in is now turned over to pasture, and the structure, although still 'mutilated', is clearly visible. The mutilation was, apparently, the work of 'an inquisitive miner' around 1890.

The gallery can be traced for 7m but it is so ruinous that it is almost impossible to say how long it was: one transversely set stone could be the backstone. The rear of the cairn has also been greatly interfered with, which means that that too is of indeterminate length. The court is in much better condition than the gallery, but is still quite ruined. There is enough of each arm present to determine that the north-facing court would have been about 7m across. The western arm has the tallest remaining stone, which is a little over 1m tall. Around the outside of the monument several stones can be seen that probably define the kerb.

Despite its poor condition there is one interesting feature that makes the site worth visiting: the monument is built on a small shelf that projects northwards from the north-west-facing hillside. Compared to the surrounding hillside this platform's presence seems a little too fortuitous, so perhaps it may have been constructed, or at least enhanced, just to accommodate the tomb. If this is the case then it raises the questions of why do that and why do it here? The view to the north is spectacular and looking south-west Knocklayd Mountain appears to sit on top of a large flat area on the next hill in that direction and it is this landscape effect that could have been the driving force behind choosing this location.

Mini-Gazetteer – 1.6km NW there is a standing stone at *Cross*. 5.1km SSE there is a standing stone at *Ballyvennaght*. 9.9km WSW there is a standing stone at *Ballylig*. 14.1km S there is a passage tomb at *Cloghs*.

Ticloy – The Stone House
Portal Tomb
Grid Ref: D 232 118 (Sheet 9)

Directions: *From Carnlough head south-east on the A42 towards Ballymena. 2km after passing the B97 to Glenarm you will come to a crossroads. Bear right and take the next right-hand turn. Follow this road for 2km where you should see the top of this tomb over a field wall to the left. Access is via a farm track adjacent to it.*

This is a chunky monument. It is also a rather ugly one! Most portal tombs use elegant and impressively large stones, while this one seems to have been made from the largest, roughest stones the builders could lay their hands on.

Most of the monument's structure appears to be present at first sight. One of the portal stones has fallen down and lies in the entrance. There is a small, low stone just to one side of the upright portal stone that seems to be the remains of a small court or *façade*. As the site is in an area with some impressive court tombs, this tomb may have

Ticloy portal tomb with Slemish on the horizon.

been built by court tomb builders moving on to a new type of tomb and retaining a little bit of their heritage.

Early drawings and reports of the site mention a second structure to the rear of the tomb. This could have been a second portal tomb or a small cist that was once incorporated into the monument's long cairn. A large stone that can be seen in a nearby wall is probably the roofstone to this missing chamber.

The location is south-facing and offers fine views over the valley below and Slemish Mountain sits nicely on the horizon, giving the site a strong point of focus.

Mini-Gazetteer – 2.5km ESE there is a court tomb at ***Antynanum***. 8.4km E there is a standing stone at ***Goakstown***. 10.4km WNW there is a stone pair at ***Lisnamanny***. 13.5km SW there is a court tomb at ***Ballymarlagh***.

Toberbile
Standing Stone
Grid Ref: D 085 372 (Sheet 5)

Directions: *From Armoy follow the A44 north towards Ballycastle. 6km from Armoy you pass a quarry on the left-hand side of the road. Take the next right-hand turn and continue south for 1.5km, where you will see the stone in a field to your left behind an abandoned farmhouse. If you reach a crossroads you have gone 300m too far.*

Toberbile standing stone.

This large standing stone is one of many that try to encircle Knocklayd Mountain. It stands in a gently sloping field at the base of Knocklayd, so naturally the mountain dominates the site. Only an old, abandoned farmhouse and a few new houses interrupt the views to the west.

The stone is 3m tall, over 1m wide at its base and 60cm thick. The stone's axis is aligned roughly east–west, pointing to (or away from) the top of Knocklayd, but from this close the cairn on top of the mountain is not visible. The dimensions of the stone mean that when it is viewed from the north or south it looks very large, while looking very slender and delicate from the east or west.

Mini-Gazetteer – 1km NE there is a standing stone at *Ballylig*. 5.2km W there is a court tomb at *Carnanmore*. 8.8km NW there is a passage tomb at *Lemnagh Beg*. 11.4km ENE there is a standing stone at *Crockanore*.

Tobergill – The Craigs
Stone Circle
Grid Ref: J 208 905 (Sheet 14)

Directions: *From Antrim take the B95 west towards Doagh, pass under the motorway and into Parkgate. Turn left in Parkgate and continue for 3.5km until you reach a crossroad. Turn left here and then up the first farm track on the right. Ask for access at the first house on the left.*

Tobergill 'stone circle'.

Although this site is described as a stone circle it is probably the remains of a court tomb. The monument is in a state of disarray with only a handful of the stones remaining set in the ground. The west side is open and was presumably the entrance to the court. A large set stone and a fallen stone of similar size flank this gap. From these two large stones the few remaining stones decrease in height.

Walking from the farmyard to the site you pass by a rock face that is probably the quarry from where the stones of this site were taken. Being able to identify the quarry site for a monument's stones is quite rare.

Mini-Gazetteer – 1.9km N there is a court tomb at **Browndod**. 9km SE there is a passage tomb at **Craigarogan**. 13.8km SE there is a court tomb at **Ballyutoag**. 15km ENE there is a standing stone at **Ballygowan**.

Tornagrough – Standing Stones Hill
Stone Pair
Grid Ref: J 252 743 (Sheet 15)

Directions: *Directions for this site are quite complicated, so using an OS map is recommended. From the west side of Belfast take the B38 west towards Glenavy, turning off onto the B154 towards Dundrod. Take the first right and then turn left at the t-junction. 400m after you pass a disused quarry/lake you reach a gate on the right-hand side. The stones are on top of the*

One of the fallen stones at Tornagrough.

hill to the north-east. The ground between the gate and the hilltop is very disturbed and boggy, so caution is advisable.

As the hill that these stones stand on was named after their presence you would think that perhaps a little more care would have been taken of them. Sadly, this is not the case and both stones are now prostrate. One of them is thrown into a ditch and covered by some chain-link fencing that has collapsed onto it, while the other lies almost buried within the small broken-down enclosure formed by the aforementioned chain-link fence.

Neither stone looks as if it would have stood more than 1m tall when stood upright and set into the ground. With such a small stature it is surprising that the whole hill was named after them, so they must have been a significant place in the minds of the locals at one time.

Mini-Gazetteer – 6.4km NE there is a court tomb at ***Ballyutoag***. 10km N there is a passage tomb at ***Craigarogan***. 10km SE there is a henge at Ballynahatty (Co. Down). 11.4km NNW there is a cairn at ***Kilmakee***.

West Division – The Schoolhouse Cairn
Cairn
Grid Ref: J 347 891 (Sheet 15)

Directions: *From Junction 2 on the M2 take the A8(M) and then the A8 north. After 6km you pass the B95 to the left. Turn right at the next opportunity and continue for 5km and turn right. After 1.5km turn up a farm track and ask at the farm for directions to the cairn (there is a radio mast above the farm).*

This hilltop cairn has some very interesting features. The first of these is a modern one and is the reason behind the site's colloquial name: the foundations of a small building, a schoolhouse, can be seen on the top of the mound. Locally, the name seems to have gone out of use in recent times.

The cairn is 3m tall and around 20m in diameter. The top has been robbed out in a few places, revealing the tops of some large stones that could be from internal chamber or cists. From the top of the cairn, standing next to the Ordnance Survey trig point, the views are wonderful if you can ignore the nearby transmitter aerial.

Another interesting feature of the monument is the large ring of stones that surrounds the cairn. This enclosure is formed by two concentric rings set 1m apart, that could be the foundations to a palisade or wall that was built around the cairn at a later date and be nothing to do with the original construction. If the ring is the original kerb of the monument then the cairn was massive, at least 50m across, but its construction and diameter make this most unlikely.

The Schoolhouse Cairn at West Division.

The Three Brothers, prostrate in West Division.

Mini-Gazetteer – 3km ENE there are two artificial mounds at ***Aldoo***. 6.1km N there is a standing stone at ***Ballygowan***. 10.6km W there is a holed standing stone at ***Holestone***. 14.5km WNW there is a court tomb at ***Browndod***.

West Division – The Three Brothers
Stone Row
Grid Ref: J 338 888 (Sheet 15)

Directions: *A difficult one to find. From Carrickfergus take the B58 north for 2.5km and turn left. When you reach a t-junction turn right and then left. After 1.5km there is a farm track on the left that heads straight up the hill. These three stones are 1km up this lane.*

All three of these stones have fallen and now lie broken at the side of a farm track. They form a line 15m long aligned roughly north to south and form part of the boundary between the track and the adjoining field.

The three stones would have been very impressive when they were standing upright. Two of them are over 2m long, while the third is slightly under 2m in length.

Mini-Gazetteer – 5.8km NNE there is a standing stone at ***Ballynarry***. 6.5km N there is a standing stone at ***Ballygowan***. 10km NNW there is a court tomb at ***Ballyalbaanagh***. 13.1km W there is a stone circle at ***Tobergill***.

Looking south-west over West Torr passage tomb.

West Torr
Passage Tomb
Grid Ref: D 213 406 (Sheet 5)

Directions: *Follow the A2 east from Ballycastle for 3km until it turns sharply right at a cross-roads. Take the road that goes straight ahead at this junction and follow it for a little over 2km, taking the third road on the left. Follow this road for 4km and turn left – you should see a large aerial on the hilltop ahead surrounded by ruined buildings. Drive up to the gates below these buildings and park. The monument is on the top of this hill behind the buildings.*

This was probably the largest of Co. Antrim's passage tombs with a diameter of nearly 20m. The cairn has been completely removed leaving a disturbed kerb and exposing the passage and chamber. Most of the orthostats from the passage have been taken away, but enough remain to show that the passage was aligned to the north-east.

The chamber is of the undifferentiated type – just a widening of the passage. Most of the orthostats are granite, but the backstone of the chamber is heavily encrusted with quartzite. If the passage were aligned with the mid-summer sunrise then the shaft of sunlight along the passage would have made this stone sparkle.

The stones forming the kerb reach 2m in length and many are over 1m tall. Just outside the kerb's southern edge there is a red granite boulder, the only one of its type in the monument. Like the backstone of the chamber, this must have had special significance to the builders.

With fantastic views all around and the chance of seeing buzzards soaring overhead, not even the monument's ruined condition and the proximity of the ruined buildings detract from this site's ambience and sense of magic. The views were probably not the only thing that first attracted people to this site: the hill is actually a chalk plateau and on the slopes below the passage tomb there are many small quarries with large quantities of flint showing where the rock is exposed.

Mini-Gazetteer — 1.9km SSE there is a passage tomb at **East Torr**. 3.8km WNW there is a cairn at **Tervillin**. 6.5km W there is a stone pair at **Ballynaglogh**. 11.2km SW there is a standing stone at **Breen**.

White Park
Cairn
Grid Ref: D 023 440 (Sheet 5)

Directions: *From Ballycastle follow the A2 west towards Bushmills. 2km after the junction with the B15 coast road you will see signs for White Park Bay on the right. Park at the car park and walk down towards the beach. At the top of the first set of steps look along the dunes from the information sign and seek out the only dome-shaped feature — this is the cairn. Access is via the beach.*

The stone that protrudes from White Park cairn.

White Park Bay between Bushmills and Ballycastle is one of the most important archaeological sites in Ireland, because of its association with the production of polished axes. Above the bay are the three passage tombs in **Clegnagh**, **Lemnaghbeg** and **Magheraboy** TDs. In the middle of the dunes between the beach and the chalk cliffs stands this lone cairn, which may be a passage tomb from the above group.

The 2m tall mound has a kerb around it halfway up. This indicates that the monument is probably built on one of the many rocky outcrops that can be seen throughout the dunes. It is quite small at 5m in diameter. On the north-east side a kerbstone is set upright, but this may be a disturbed kerbstone. On the top of the mound a slab is visible that could be from the internal structure.

With the crashing of the surf on the beach and large boulders below, this is a wonderfully calm place to sit. It is far enough back from the beach that the noise from the surf covers the noise of the many visitors to this beach. However, quad bikes riding through the dunes sometimes break this peace.

Mini-Gazetteer – 1.4km E there is a passage tomb known as *The Druid Stone* at **Magheraboy**. 9.1km SE there is a standing stone at **Ballylig**. 10.6km WSW there is a standing stone at **Flower Hill**. 13.7km E there is a passage tomb at **Ballyvoy**.

Notes

Abbreviations used:

JRSAI – Journal of the Royal Society of Antiquaries of Ireland
PSAMNI – A Preliminary Survey of the Ancient Monuments of Northern Ireland
PRIA – Proceedings of the Royal Irish Academy
JRHAAI – The Journal of the Royal Historical and Archaeological Association of Ireland (later to become JRSAI)

1. Woodman, P.C., *Settlement Patterns of the Irish Mesolithic* (UJA, 1973) p.10.
2. Richie, P.R. & Scott, J.G., *The Petrological Identification of Axes from Scotland* (CBA Research Report 67, 1988).
3. Clark, A.F., *The Neolithic of Kent: a review* (1982).
4. Cooney, G., & Mandal, S., *Irish Stone Axe Project* (Wordwell Press Ltd, 1998) p.119.
5. Blake Whelan, C., 'The Flint Industry of the Northern Irish Raised Beach', *Journal of the Royal Anthropolgical Institute of Great Britain and Ireland* vol.60, p.180.
6. PSAMNI (H.M. Stationery Office, 1940) p.35.
7. Borlase, William C., *The Dolmens of Ireland* (Chapman & Hall, 1897) p.264.
8. PSAMNI (H.M. Stationery Office, 1940) p.28.
9. Herity M., *The Finds From Irish Court Tombs* (PRIA, 1987) pp135, 253.
10. PSAMNI (H.M. Stationery Office, 1940) p.29.
11. Anthony Weir – personal comment.
12. Borlase, William C., *The Dolmens of Ireland* (Chapman & Hall, 1897) p.263.
13. Mallory, J.P., & McNeill, T.E., *The Archaeology of Ulster* (Institute of Irish Studies, 1991) p.45.
14. Wood-Martin, *Pagan Ireland An Archaeological Sketch* (Longmans & Co., 1895) p.312.
15. *ibid.*
16. D'Arcy, S.A., '"Holed"-Stone at Cushendall, Co. Antrim' *JRSAI*, vol.60, pt 2, p.192.
17. PSAMNI (H.M. Stationery Office, 1940) p.15.
18. Evans, Estyn, *Prehistoric and Early Christian Ireland: A Guide* (Batsford, 1966) p. 47.
19. PSAMNI (H.M. Stationery Office, 1940) p.9.
20. PSAMNI (H.M. Stationery Office, 1940) p.8.

21. Borlase, William C., *The Dolmens of Ireland* (Chapman & Hall, 1897) p.260.

22. Mogey, J.M., *The 'Druid Stone', Ballintoy, Co. Antrim* (UJA, 1941) pp49–56.

23. PSAMNI (H.M. Stationery Office, 1940) p.4.

24. Collins, A., *A Sand-Dune Site at the White Rocks, County Antrim* (UJA, vol. 40, 1977) p.24.

25. Northern Ireland Sites and Monuments Record, SMR number: ANT 008:008

26. Personal comment from the landowner.

27. http://ads.ahds.ac.uk/catalogue/search/fr.cfm?rcn=NISMR-ANT014:006 (21 March 2008)

28. Tomb, J.J., & Davies, O., *Further Urns From Ballymacaldrack* (UJA, 1941) pp63–66.

29. Borlase, William C., *The Dolmens of Ireland* (Chapman & Hall, 1897) p.265.

30. Gray, William, 'Cromlechs in counties of Antrim and Down', *Journal of the Royal Archaeological Society*, 1884, p. 361.

31. *ibid.*

32. Borlase, William C., *The Dolmens of Ireland* (Chapman & Hall, 1897) p.265.

33. Wood-Martin, *Pagan Ireland An Archaeological Sketch* (Longmans & Co, 1895) p.272.

34. Borlase, William C., *The Dolmens of Ireland* (Chapman & Hall, 1897) p.265.

35. Gray, William, 'Cromlechs in counties of Antrim and Down', *Journal of the Royal Archaeological Society*, 1884, p. 361.

36. Williams, B.B., *A Passage Tomb at Craigs, County Antrim* (UJA, 1987) pp129–130.

37. *ibid.* p.133.

38. PSAMNI (H.M. Stationery Office, 1940) p. 27.

39. Borlase, William C., *The Dolmens of Ireland* (Chapman & Hall, 1897) p.266.

40. *ibid.*

41. Gray, William, 'Cromlechs in counties of Antrim and Down', *Journal of the Royal Archaeological Society*, 1884, p.360.

42. Borlase, William C., *The Dolmens of Ireland* (Chapman & Hall, 1897) p.266.

43. 'Excursion Through the Valley of the Braid', *Journal of the Royal Archaeological Society*, 1883, p.177.

44. Brian McElherron (part of the clearance team) – personal comment.

45. Herity, Michael, *Finds From Irish Court Tombs* (PRIA, 1987) p.168.

46. Borlase, William C., *The Dolmens of Ireland* (Chapman & Hall, 1897) p.268.

47. *ibid.*

48. PSAMNI (H.M. Stationery Office, 1940) p.38.

49. Northern Ireland Sites and Monuments Record.

50. Herity, Michael, *Finds From Irish Court Tombs* (PRIA, 1987) p.176.

51. *Journal of the Royal Archaeological Society* (vol. 35, 1905) p.289.

52. FourWinds, Tom, *Monu-Mental About Prehistoric Dublin* (Nonsuch Publishing, 2006) p.81.

53. De Valera, R. & Ó Nualláin, S., *Survey of the Megalithic Tombs of Ireland, Volume IV* (The Stationery Office, 1982) p.3.

54. De Valera, R., & Ó Nualláin, S., *Survey of the Megalithic Tombs of Ireland, Volume II* (The Stationery Office, 1964) p.42.

55. Mallory, J.P., & McNeill, T.E., *The Archaeology of Ulster* (Institute of Irish Studies, Queen's University Belfast, 1991) p.64.

56. Powell, T., *Excavation of the Megalithic Chambered cairn at Dyffryn Ardudwy, Merioneth, Wales* (Archaelogia, vol.104, 1973).

57. Weir, Anthony, *Early Ireland: A Field Guide* (Blackstaff Press, 1980) p.131.

58. Gray, W., 'Cromlechs in counties of Antrim and Down', *Journal of the Royal Archaeological Society*, 1884, p.362.

59. Unknown source – possibly Gray's *Guide to Belfast* (1832).

60. Borlase, William C., *The Dolmens of Ireland* (Chapman & Hall, 1897) p.270.

61. Collins, A., 'Dooey's Cairn, Ballymacaldrack, County Antrim' (*UJA*, vol.39, 1976) p.1.

62. *ibid.* (p.5)

63. Daives, *Excavations at the Horned Cairn at Ballymarlagh, Co. Antrim* (UJA – vol.12, 1948).

64. Evans, Estyn, *Prehistoric and Early Christian Ireland: A Guide* (Batsford, 1966) p.44.

65. PSAMNI (H.M. Stationery Office, 1940) p.53.

66. Herity, M., *The Finds From Irish Court Tombs* (PRIA, 1987) p.158.

67. Evans, Estyn, *Prehistoric and Early Christian Ireland: A Guide* (Batsford, 1966) p.44.

68. Ezekiel: 38

69. Lethbridge, T.C., *Gogmagog: The Buried Gods* (Routledge & Kegan Paul Ltd, 1957).

70. Herity, M., *The Finds From Irish Court Tombs* (PRIA, 1987) pp175-179.

71. Borlase, William C., *The Dolmens of Ireland* (Chapman & Hall, 1897) p.259.

72. PSAMNI (H.M. Stationery Office, 1940) p.4.

73. JRHAAI (University Press, Dublin, 1884) p.360.

74. Northern Irish Sites and Monuments Record.

75. Joussaume, Roger, *Dolmens For The Dead* (Guild Publishing, 1988) p.43.

76. PSAMNI (H.M. Stationery Office, 1940) p.47.

77. Lawlor, H.C., *Ulster: Its Archaeology and Antiquities* (R. Carswell & Sons, Ltd, 1928) p.20.

78. PSAMNI (H.M. Stationery Office, 1940) p.22.

79. Wood-Martin, *Pagan Ireland An Archaeological Sketch* (Longmans & Co., 1895) p.272.

80. Borlase, William C., *The Dolmens of Ireland* (Chapman & Hall, 1897) p.260.

81. PSAMNI (H.M. Stationery Office, 1940) p.28.

82. *ibid.*

83. Taken from the information board at the site.

84. http://www.irishmegaliths.org.uk/zKillyglen.htm (Feb. 2008)

85. Gray, William, 'Cromlechs in counties of Antrim and Down', *Journal of the Royal Archaeological Society*, 1884, p.360.

86. Mogey, J.M., *The 'Druid Stone', Ballintoy, Co. Antrim* (UJA, 1941) pp49-56.

87. PSAMNI (H.M. Stationery Office, 1940) p.11.

88. PSAMNI (H.M. Stationery Office, 1940) p.8.